No Surrender!
Women's Suffrage in Nottinghamshire

Contributors:
Val Wood
Sian Trafford
Mo Cooper
Anne Darby
Rowena Edlin-White

Edited by Rowena Edlin-White

Compiled by Nottingham Women's History Group

Published with the generous help of Nottinghamshire Local History Association

No Surrender!
Women's Suffrage in Nottinghamshire

© Nottingham Women's History Group

ISBN: 978-1-900074-31-5

*All rights reserved.
No part of this publication may be reproduced
in any form, or by any means, without permission
of the Authors and Publisher.*

Published by *Smallprint*
11, Frederick Avenue, Carlton NG4 1HP
2018

Printed by Unwin Print, Farnsfield, Notts. 01623-882627

Nottingham Women's History Group

Celebrate, promote and research the contribution of women to Nottingham's history

Introduction

The women's suffrage campaign was a single-issue political campaign which began in the 1860s and continued until women gained full enfranchisement in 1928. The main focus of this book is the Edwardian women's suffrage campaign in Nottinghamshire. The campaign is outlined in the form of a narrative account supplemented by some of the local campaigners' stories. It is not a complete record; we seek simply to create a starting point for the reader in anticipation that there will be further research and different interpretations in the future. The history of women's suffrage in the provinces is only starting to emerge and raises our awareness of the significant number of women who committed themselves to the campaign over and above the household names synonymous with the movement.

The campaign for the vote was passionately fought in Nottingham with large out-of-door suffrage meetings being held on the Forest Recreation Ground and in the Market-place which attracted crowds of up to three and four thousand during 1908. Frequent political meetings took place in the main city meeting halls, the Mechanics Institute, the Albert Hall and the Congregational Mission Hall on East Circus Street. Leading suffragette and suffragist leaders Emmeline Pankhurst, Emmeline Pethick Lawrence, Millicent Fawcett, and Adela, Sylvia and Christabel Pankhurst were regular speakers in Nottingham during the period from 1907 to 1914.

The women suffrage supporters in the city aligned themselves to two main female suffrage societies in Nottingham, the National Union of Women's Suffrage Societies (NUWSS) and the breakaway Women's Social and Political Union (WSPU). From 1908 many women actively supported the

Church League for Women's Suffrage (CLWS) when a branch was established in the city. The city suffragettes and suffragists participated in demonstrations in London, petitioned and lobbied members of Parliament, held meetings, sold newspapers in the Market-place, and some members of the Nottingham WSPU undertook militant action, were arrested, imprisoned and underwent hunger strikes and forced feeding.

The research for the book has drawn on a range of both primary resource material and some, albeit limited, personal diaries and letters, the detail of which is used to support the narrative and also to provide further reading. The most interesting finding to date is the *extent* of the women's suffrage campaign in both the city and certain parts of the county, and its relevance to both the national campaign and to understanding feminist networks in Nottinghamshire in the early 20th Century.

We hope you enjoy reading this book.

Val Wood
Nottingham Women's History Group
February 2018

Background to the Women's Suffrage Campaign in Nottingham

Women and Chartism
Chartism, founded in 1837 to promote political democracy, was supported by many working class women in Nottingham. This involved women taking an active, public and often turbulent part in meetings and street demonstrations. In 1838, they set up their own organisation, the Nottingham Female Political Union. In addition to campaigning for the vote and suffrage for both sexes, women also agitated locally on food prices; one of their campaigning tactics being to exhort women to buy only from shops that supported the people's cause.

Female-only Friendly Societies were noted in Nottingham and the county in the early years of the 19th Century. In 1803, there were twenty-three registered societies for women with a membership of 1,644.[1] These numbers increased significantly during the 1830s and 1840s in response to women's concern following the implementation of the 1834 Poor Law Amendment Act. Friendly societies provided benefits to members as a right, in return for regular subscriptions. To receive financial assistance from a society, to be 'on the club' or to make a claim 'on the box' did not carry the same stigma as seeking support from the local parish or receiving handouts from charitable sources. With improving economic conditions in the 1850s, the Chartist movement declined and working women looked towards the establishment of their own Trade and Friendly Societies.

Nottingham's First Feminists
The aims of first-wave feminists were to create awareness of women's public (legal) and private (in the home) oppression. These women largely responded to specific injustice they themselves had suffered but also raised awareness of the need for better working conditions and wages for working-class women. While seeking to gain better education and employment, for middle-class women their campaigning would, at a later date, be linked to demands for their right to vote.

---

[1] O'Neill, J. (2001) *In the Club, Female Friendly Societies in Nottinghamshire*. Trent Valley History Group.

Mary Ann Radcliffe (1746-1818) was probably the first Nottingham woman to address in print the issue of women's work and poverty. Not to be confused with her name-sake, the author of Gothic novels, Radcliffe was born Mary Ann Clayton and baptised at St Nicholas' Church, Nottingham on 18 June 1746. She was the daughter of James Clayton, a merchant, and his wife Sarah Blatherwick. Her father died when she was four, leaving her an heiress. She tells her life story in *The Memoirs of Mrs Mary Ann Radcliffe in Familiar Letters to Her Female Friend* (1810): she was educated at the Bar Convent at York, but eloped with Joseph Radcliffe when she was fifteen and had eight children in quick succession. Forced to sell her estates to pay her husband's mounting debts, by 1783 she was seeking employment as a house-keeper, governess and milliner, and she managed to earn enough to educate her three sons. In 1799 she published *The Female Advocate; or An Attempt to Recover the Rights of Women from Male Usurpation*, arguing that men's incursion into work such as millinery deprived women of work and forced them into prostitution; she also argued that the lack of proper education deprived women of respectable employment. Her husband died in 1804 and by 1810, in failing health, she was being supported by her friend Mrs Ferrier in Edinburgh, where in 1818, she died.

Ann Taylor Gilbert (1782-1866) represents some aspects of feminism in her writing and actions in support of women and other minority groups in the early Victorian period. Ann and her sister Jane Taylor (1783-1824) became famous for their collection of poems and hymns for young children *Original Poems for Infant Minds* (1804 & 1805) and *Rhymes for the Nursery* (1806). In her poem 'Remonstrance' published in 1810, Ann promotes the role of women in supporting their husbands but also their need to have a domestic life separate from men. The concept of separate spheres was vigorously promoted in the 19th century as the ideal model for relations between men and women, particularly for the middle and higher social classes. In 1813 Ann married Rev Joseph Gilbert who became Minister of Friar Lane Chapel. She set up the Nottingham Ladies Society for the Relief of Negro Slaves, campaigning as part of the anti-slavery movement in Britain and was involved in the establishment of the free library in Nottingham. She also established one of the earliest refuges for 'unfortunate women' in Nottingham in the 1830s.

In the late Victorian period, middle-class women in Nottingham (often the wives and daughters of professional men, factory owners and lace manufacturers) were increasingly involved in a range of charitable activities. Female philanthropy was mainly organised around helping the poor and it can be argued that this enabled women to participate in their local communities. It took the form of visiting the homes of poor women and the institutions, both public and private, that provided for women, for example, the workhouse.

The life and work of Henrietta Carey (1845-1925) demonstrates the increased involvement in public life by Nottingham women. Henrietta helped to establish the Nottingham Town and County Social Guild in 1875 which undertook many charitable works. The Guild provided blanket loans, ran a girls' club and a cheap dinner scheme for children. She also established a residential hostel for women working in the city, a club for working women and a dining hall in Trinity Square. Henrietta was very much involved with the National Union of Women Workers which was formed in 1895 to provide a platform for women who worked mostly in a voluntary capacity. Their aim was "the social, moral and religious elevation of their own sex." The first conference of the National Union was held in Nottingham in 1896 and discussed a range of topics of significance to women including a debate on Parliamentary Suffrage led by Mrs Fawcett and Mrs Sandford.[2]

Another locally-based woman was Lady Laura Ridding (1849-1939) who was a long-standing supporter of women's suffrage and, like Henrietta, one of the founders of the National Union of Women Workers. Laura was the second wife of George Ridding, the first Bishop of Southwell, and together they were very active in social projects for women and girls.

Nottingham has a long tradition of nonconformity in respect of religion and many of the women associated with the Unitarian, Methodist, Congregational and Quaker religious groups were active in their support for women's causes

---

[2] Report of the 1896 Conference.

and the fight for equality and universal suffrage. Mary Clara Sophia Neal (1860-1944) was a regular lecturer at Nottingham Labour Church in her early years before she relocated to London.[3]

Religion gave women status within the community and allowed them to gain administrative skills. Women tended to undertake the teaching at the Sunday schools and it was their job to educate the next generation into religion as well as to teach the basic skills of reading and writing. Hannah Guilford (1840-1936), a teacher at High Pavement Sunday School, was elected as Chairman of the Chapel Council in 1904, a position normally occupied by a man. Hannah was also elected to sit on the Nottingham School Board in 1892 and remained there until 1904; when it was taken over by the City Council she was co-opted onto the Education Committee. A less prestigious position was to serve as a Poor Law Guardian[4] to which Hannah's sister, Sarah, was elected. The two women and their married sister, Ann Cowen, were to become active suffragists.

Two other Unitarian families connected through marriage, the Brownswords and Dowsons, were active in the fight for universal suffrage. Anderson Brownsword, later to become Sheriff of Nottingham, chaired suffrage meetings in the 1870s, and his daughter Helena (1866-1964) was to become very involved in the women's suffrage movement in the late 1890s, working with her mother-in-law Alice Dowson (1844-1927), both of them engaged with social and political issues.

In the wider county Emily Manners (1857-1934), a Quaker, was the first woman to be elected a Poor Law Guardian in Mansfield and at the time of her death in 1934 was a Justice of the Peace. In 1903 she was on the National Executive committee of the Women's Suffrage Societies representing Mansfield.

The development of the women's campaign for enfranchisement began in the middle of the 19th century and Nottingham, having a reputation for radicalism, was an important centre for the movement. The campaign for the vote grew

---

[3] According to Peter Wyncoll (1985) this was a congregation which met in Hyson Green, often attracting a crowd of 1,800 active socialists in the 1890s.
[4] The Local Government Act of 1894 allowed some propertied women to vote and stand as Poor Law Guardians.

out of the earlier 19th century movements calling for improved welfare, education and employment for women. The renewed activity for the suffrage in Nottingham began in 1866 and the first women's suffrage petition was submitted to the House of Commons in 1869. In 1866, forty-nine women had signed a petition, but it wasn't until 1869 and 1870 that suffrage petitions from Nottingham were actually presented in the House of Commons. Nottingham saw frequent meetings addressed by both male and female speakers and further petitions were initiated.

In 1871 a Nottingham committee of the London National Society for Women's Suffrage was founded, the president being Rev Richard A. Armstrong, a preacher at High Pavement Chapel. The Honourable Secretary was Elizabeth Sunter who resided at 40 Bilbie Street,[5] Nottingham. This committee was an umbrella organisation for a variety of groups in the city, for example the Women's Temperance Society and the National Union of Women Workers. Margaret Bright Lucas (1818-1890), a Quaker and President of the British Women's Temperance Society from 1877, attended regular suffrage meetings in Nottingham which had a well-established temperance following in the late Victorian period. Margaret's sister, Priscilla, was also active in the suffrage movement.

In 1872 Nottingham's committee was associated with the new Central Committee of the National Society for Women's Suffrage which was the first national group in Britain to campaign for women's right to vote and laid the foundations of the women's suffrage movement. The first executive committee of the National Society included Frances Power Cobbe, Priscilla Bright McLaren, Agnes Garrett and Lilias Ashworth Hallett. A wealthy woman, Lilias Hallett funded suffrage meetings in Nottingham and Grantham in 1875.[6] There seems to have been a lull in activity between 1872 and 1880, although the diaries of Alice Dowson[7] frequently mention the women's suffrage cause during the 1870s, indicating that interested women in Nottingham were aware of events pertaining to the cause and were also, perhaps, in contact with activists from elsewhere.

---

[5] Bilbie Street was located in the area where Nottingham Trent University is sited. All that remains is the narrow cut–through called Bilbie Walk. Elizabeth Sunter taught at Peoples College in the 1850s and later opened a private school for girls.
[6] Elizabeth Crawford (2001), p 260.
[7] Meynell, A. (1989) *What Grandmother Said: the Life of Alice Dowson 1844-1927*.

In 1874 the Central Committee introduced a yearly subscription of one shilling. Lydia Becker became secretary of the Central Committee in 1881 and additional executive members included Millicent Fawcett.[8] According to Elizabeth Crawford's book, *The Women's Suffrage Movement*, Ann Cowen represented Nottingham in 1885 on the executive committee of the National Society for Women's Suffrage which met in London.[9]

By 1880, however, Nottingham had again entered the fray with meetings on consecutive days in November of that year, the first at the Morley Club in Shakespeare Street and the second at the Co-operative Hall in Sandford Street. There were other well-attended meetings during this period, for example a meeting held on 31st March 1880 in the school room of the Baptist Chapel, Woodborough Road, when Alice Cliff Scatcherd[10] from Morley in Leeds, lectured on 'Women's Suffrage, What will it do for us?' led to proposals for petitions in favour of the principles of women's suffrage being adopted.[11] In Nottingham, a petition from 885 women householders in Sherwood, Market, St Ann's, Forest and part of Manvers and Mapperley Wards was presented to Parliament in 1881 by the town's Member of Parliament, Arnold Morley.

There also followed a series of meetings in locations as diverse as drawing rooms and school rooms, culminating in a 'Grand Demonstration' on 30 November 1880. The term refers to a show of mass support for the inclusion of the enfranchisement of women in the 1884 Reform Bill. Speakers at the Nottingham 'demonstration'[12] included women who held a national profile as activists in the suffrage campaign: Helen Taylor (1831-1907), Caroline Biggs (1840-1889), Helena Downing (1845-1885), Jessie Craigen (1835-1899) and Lady Florence Harberton (1844-1911). Representing Nottingham at this meeting was Alice Dowson.

---

[8] Spartacus Educational Website.
[9] Crawford (2001) p 102.
[10] Liberal philanthropist and radical suffragist (1842-1906).
[11] *Nottingham Evening Post*, 16.12.1881.
[12] *Nottingham Evening Post* advertisement: "A Great Demonstration of Women to be held at the Albert Hall on Tuesday Evening, 30th November 1880 in support of the bill for the removal of the electoral disabilities of women – seats will be free for women and gentlemen will be charged 2/6 to sit in the gallery."

Nottingham Women's Suffrage Society

On 15 December 1881 the first annual meeting of the members of the Nottingham branch of the Women's Suffrage Society took place at the Exchange Rooms, Nottingham. This meeting was presided over by the ex-Sheriff of Nottingham, Mr H.S. Cropper, as the Mayor was unable to attend. The *Nottingham Evening Post* provided an account on 16 December 1881, printing the full content of the annual report as read by the Honorary Secretary of the society, the aforementioned Ann Cowen. The AGM elected a new committee which, as shown below, included several men. The annual report provides an interesting account of the activities of supporters for women's suffrage in the town.

Committee members of the Nottingham Branch of the Women's Suffrage Society in 1881

Mrs Butler
Mrs Ann Cowen
Mr E. S. Cowen
Mr H. S. Cropper (Sheriff/Mayor)
Miss H. Guilford
Mr and Mrs Jesse Hind
Miss A. Smith
Miss Elizabeth Sunter
Mrs Teschemacher
Mr J.W. Windley
Mrs Shearer (London representative aka Miss Downing)
Mrs Brook (Newark)
Miss Louisa Wright (Mansfield)
Mrs D'Hersant
Mrs Samuels

Over the next few years, this Annual General Meeting of the Nottingham Women's Suffrage Society was the main rallying point for the suffrage cause in Nottingham, inviting various inspirational and motivating speakers from other societies. The campaign continued in this vein, with meetings and rallies in keeping with the NWSS adherence to peaceful and constitutional means of protest. However, meetings were frequently disrupted or even prevented from happening at all by the rowdy, threatening and intimidating behaviour of youths and men.

It is important to remember when considering the composition of the Nottingham suffrage society at this period in time that demand for the vote was mainly sought *via* constitutional means – by engaging a sympathetic MP to take a resolution forward into Parliament. The Nottingham Corporation (the Town Council) in the early 1880s was composed of a significant number of councillors of Liberal persuasion, and many women were actively involved in the Liberal Federation at this time despite not having any right to vote. After the 1884 Reform Act failed to acknowledge female voting rights, a National Women's Liberal Federation was established with local branches springing up, including in Nottingham. It was Liberal women activists who were to form the core of the emerging new suffrage group in the 1890s, many of whom were engaged in philanthropic work and associated with the non-conformist religious families in Nottingham. In 1896 a National Union of Practical Suffragists was formed within the Women's Liberal Federation which sought to "induce the Women's Liberal Associations to work for no Liberal candidate who would vote against women's suffrage in the House of Commons."

In 1897 the National Union of Women's Suffrage Societies (NUWSS) was established under the leadership of Millicent Garrett Fawcett. The motto of the new organisation was 'Faith, Perseverance and Patience'. The Nottingham Women's Suffrage Society affiliated to the NUWSS in 1898 and held its first meeting chaired by Helena Dowson, the Honorary Secretary being Alice Dowson. Around this time Helena joined the executive committee of the National Union of Women's Suffrage Societies[13] and her name and actions will be noted throughout this book as a leading suffragist of the NUWSS in Nottingham.

---

[13] Crawford (2001), pp 173-4.

The Edwardian Suffrage campaign in Nottingham 1901-1914

In terms of suffrage activity, the early years of the 20th century appear to have been relatively quiet both in Nottingham and nationally; but with the creation in 1903 of a new suffrage society, the Women's Social and Political Union (WSPU), formed in Manchester at the home of Emmeline Pankhurst, things began to change.

The Nottingham Suffrage Society had, as noted above, affiliated to the National Union of Women's Suffrage Societies (NUWSS) in 1898. The aim of the NUWSS was to support a Private Member's Bill for women's suffrage based on the premise of equal voting rights for men and women under existing laws, which at this time required property qualifications, clearly excluding many women - and men. The NUWSS adopted a non-party policy, offering support in the constituencies during elections to candidates who supported votes for women, holding meetings and campaigning for the vote, which was referred to as a 'constitutionalist' approach.

The rise of the WSPU

In 1903, frustration and disappointment at the slow pace of change in gaining the vote for women led to the founding of the Women's Social and Political Union by Emmeline Pankhurst and her supporters, not least her daughters Adela, Christabel and Sylvia. The formation of the WSPU arose from dissatisfaction within the existing women's political organisations. According to Sandra Holton (2015), Emmeline Pankhurst came to "question the value of private members' women's suffrage bills, after watching the talking out of such a measure in May 1905, amid ridicule and ribaldry in Parliament."[14] The motto of the WSPU was 'Deeds not Words', their campaign colours purple, green and white, and their newspaper succinctly called *Votes for Women*. In the early period from 1903 to 1906 the WSPU was mainly active in the North-West around the Manchester area, with a small group in London. They were not the only organisation in the region; there was, for example, the Lancashire and Cheshire Textile and Other Workers' Representation Committee, which

---

[14] *Oxford Dictionary of National Biography.*

had a solid base amongst women trade unionists. This committee formulated its demand in terms of 'womanhood suffrage', the vote for all adult women and the call for a fully democratic franchise, a demand which was more in keeping with that of many labour and socialist supporters. In 1906, following successful local campaigning in and around the North-West, Emmeline and Christabel Pankhurst decided to move the WSPU headquarters to London and commence a campaign to gain support from the provinces, establishing branches by placing a local organiser from their ranks within key cities.

The WSPU quickly established a branch in Nottingham, as is evident in a letter from the Nottingham branch to the local Trade Union Council in 1906 asking for help in their campaign to secure votes for women, According to Peter Wyncoll, the letter received no response, it simply lay on the table.[15] The secretary of the Nottingham WSPU branch was Miss C. M. Burgis who was living at 21 Chaucer Street. 'May' Burgis, as she was known, was supported by Dorothy Pethick who was employed as Superintendent of Girls' Clubs in Nottingham and was the sister of Emmeline Pethick Lawrence, one of the founders of the WSPU. In terms of who comprised the membership of the Nottingham WSPU, this has been hard to gauge: May Burgis was a Nottingham teacher and Leonora Shaw, also a founding member, the wife of a Nottingham University College science lecturer. Working class women appear to be unrepresented despite the high proportion of working women in the city at this time.[16] This is not to suggest that working-class women were not interested in the campaign for the vote; women were active in other organisations such as the Independent Labour Party (ILP) and the Clarion Club.[17] By 1896 the ILP had 1,000 members in Nottingham (both men and women) and two club rooms. However, the organisation of women into trade unions was thwarted both by the Nottingham Trades Union Council and the skilled men in the city's traditional industries of lace and hosiery trade unions.

---

[15] Wyncoll, P. (1985) *The Nottingham Labour Movement 1880-1939,* p 95.
[16] By 1906, 67.7% of the total female population of Nottingham was in employment.
[17] The Clarion Club was formed in 1895 as a Socialist cycling club - at weekends hundreds of 'Clarionettes' on bicycles would set off into the countryside holding political meetings and distributing socialist literature.

Paid organisers from the London offices of the WSPU were put in place. The first in Nottingham was Rachel Barrett in 1908,[18] who also held a regional remit to organise and support the development of branches further afield. The organisers were paid £2 per week. The Midlands regional organiser was Gladice Keevil who was based in Birmingham. In Nottingham during this period, both the NUWSS and the WSPU established themselves, opening shops and campaigning locally. The NUWSS shop was located in Regent Chambers, 54 Long Row, near the Market-place, while the WSPU had shops in various locations at 6 Carlton Street and later, 30 Bridlesmith Gate and 31 Derby Road. In addition, the Nottingham Women's Suffrage Society ran a library, lending out books for a penny a week.

Meetings and Demonstrations

The Liberal Party's success in the 1906 General Election galvanised the NUWSS into greater activity, but was followed by a series of disappointments for suffrage campaigners as two further Private Member suffrage bills were talked out of Parliament in 1907 and 1908. A large demonstration took place in London on 9 February 1907 organised by the NUWSS, when women from all over the country were invited to join a United Procession of Women. It was estimated that there were 3,000 women present, representing forty groups, led by Millicent Fawcett.

On the day of the procession, which started in Hyde Park and ended in the Strand, inclement weather led to this becoming known as the 'Mud March' due to the state of the women's shoes and skirt hems. There were few WSPU supporters at this particular demonstration - 'suffragettes'[19] as they were now becoming called - as the Women's Liberal Federation had refused to join the demonstration if the WSPU was invited. As the leader of the NUWSS Millicent Fawcett proclaimed to her supporters, "Prove your earnestness in a manner both reflective and constitutional." [20]

In Nottingham, the WSPU organised a meeting at University College, in conjunction with the Students' Association, where Christabel Pankhurst was scheduled to speak on 28 November 1907. This meeting was blocked by the

---

[18] Rachel Barrett (1874-1953) joined the WSPU in 1906 and in 1910 was appointed WSPU organiser for Wales. Morrell (2004) *Oxford Dictionary of National Biography*.
[19] Coined by the *Daily Mail* newspaper in 1906.
[20] Hawksley, L. (2013) *March, Women, March*, p 139.

University as it was deemed to be a political rather than an educational event and it had to be relocated to the Baptist Church on Woodborough Road.[21] According to Richard Whitmore, Nottingham University College reversed its decision after several governors resigned.[22]

The next WSPU meeting in Nottingham took place on 2 December 1907. Addressed by Christabel Pankhurst and Emmeline Pethick Lawrence, it was held at the Mechanics Institute[23] as part of a national campaign aimed at convincing provincial women to participate in the WSPU. The meeting proved to be particularly volatile: according to the Nottingham newspapers, "Scenes of indescribable disorder" ensued as an unruly crowd hijacked the meeting; mice were let loose on the platform, bawdy songs were sung and Miss Pankhurst and her colleagues struggled for more than an hour to make themselves heard.[24] Some sources suggest that university students were responsible. This is how the *Nottingham Evening Post* of 3 December 1907 reported the meeting:

> The gathering, convened by the Women's Social and Political Union was held at the Mechanics' Large Hall, Miss Christabel Pankhurst, Mrs Pethick Lawrence and Miss Una Dugdale, all prominent in the present crusade, being the speakers. Admission to the greater part of the building was by ticket, but the opposition was clearly organised and the moment the doors were opened at half past seven fully a hundred seats at the back of the gallery were promptly occupied by young men, many of whom were said to be students. The six rows nearest the platform were numbered and reserved but nearly everyone gave them a wide berth until late in the evening, when it became clear that nothing more tangible than yells was to be hurled at the speakers.
>
> The dourest opponent of female suffrage could not have withheld admiration for Miss Pankhurst's pluck. Dressed in a pretty shade of blue, and wearing no hat, she kept on her feet for 70 minutes, although not as many words reached the audience. Even when the platform was stormed she did not loose her nerve. She took her gruelling - one dared not say

---

[21] *Nottingham Evening Post*, 30.11.1907 & 2.12.1907.
[22] Whitmore, R. (2007) *Alice Hawkins and the Suffragette Movement in Edwardian Leiceste*r, p 169.
[23] Then on the corner of Burton Street and Leys Street.
[24] *Nottingham Evening Post*, 3.12.1907.

'like a man' but, at any rate, like a remarkably plucky woman. Her chubby face perspiring freely from her vain attempts to make herself heard, never once lost its good-humoured expression – nay, more, she even smiled at her tormentors. These gave her no chance as trumpets, rattles, whistles, and every other ear-splitting device known to Goose Fair was employed with disastrous result. Occasionally she stopped speaking for a few minutes, but these intervals of relaxation were rare, and for the most part she was declaiming her loudest – which under the circumstances counted for very little.

At the end of the meeting, Christabel Pankhurst closed with the following words:

> "The women of Nottingham are with us, and we shall come again shortly. I have enjoyed the meeting. It will be a good advertisement, and will bring many people over to our side. The men of Nottingham had to burn the Castle before they could get votes. We shall continue our tactics."[25]

The tactics she referred to included organising large, colourful processions seeking to demonstrate the popularity of their cause, exhibitions, deputations to Parliament to coincide with each new session and the lobbying of Members of Parliament to demand the vote.

Nottingham WSPU subsequently held a second, women-only, meeting in the Circus Street Hall on 9 December 1907, when Christabel Pankhurst and Miss Aeta Lamb, a national spokesperson for the WSPU, addressed the meeting.

On 11 December 1907 the WSPU attempted to break up Asquith's meeting at the Mechanics Institute in Nottingham. Herbert Asquith, Liberal MP and Prime Minister during the period 1908-16, was antagonistic to the cause of women's suffrage. On this occasion, the authorities were so frightened by the threat of suffragette intervention, it was declared that in order for a woman to purchase a ticket for the meeting, she had to give her name and address so that

---

[25] *Nottingham Evening Post*, 3.12.1907. The reference to the Castle relates to violent demonstrations in Nottingham in the period leading up to the introduction of the 1832 Reform Bill which enfranchised some, but not all, male voters.

preliminary inquiries could be made, and her *bona-fide* had to be authenticated by two men! Even the *Nottingham Evening Post* suggested that "the elaborate precautions for excluding the suffragists make the term 'weaker sex' distinctly ironical."[26]

At a national level, however, the WSPU was experiencing internal disputes over its leadership and what some members considered to be a lack of accountability and democratic decision-making. In 1907, several prominent suffragettes and members of the WSPU executive committee, including Teresa Billington Greig and Charlotte Despard, resigned and set up the Women's Freedom League.[27] According to Hawksley (2013) they took with them a large percentage of the WSPU's membership. To date, we have found no evidence to suggest any WFL activity in Nottingham.

1907 also saw the founding of other suffrage groups, including the Men's League for Women's Suffrage which held some activities in Nottingham and, in 1909. The Church League for Women's Suffrage had established a local branch by 1913. Local activists included Rev Richard Armstrong and Rev Alan Watts, vicar of Lenton. Another key member was Rev J. M. Lloyd Thomas whose address, 'The Emancipation of Womanhood', at High Pavement Chapel on 14 November 1909 was published as a pamphlet by the WSPU.[28]

Despite the internal disputes affecting the WSPU, the local group continued to grow and it has been estimated that there was significant support in Nottingham where several meetings took place in the spring of 1908. Speakers included Christabel Pankhurst on 11 April when an estimated 450 attended to hear her speak at the Victoria Station hotel, indicating the level of local interest. A second meeting on 7 May was addressed by Emmeline Pankhurst, leader of the WSPU. Meanwhile, the Nottingham branch of the NUWSS was organising meetings mainly in the drawing rooms of local supporters, referred to as 'At Homes', suggesting the social class of the branch as middle-class women of liberal persuasion[29] who had time to devote to the cause. The group

---

[26] *Nottingham Evening Post*, 3.12.1907.
[27] Hawksley (2013), p 30.
[28] The Women's Press, 4 Clement's Inn, Strand, London W.C.
[29] In 1910 the Nottingham branch officers of the Nottingham Women's Suffrage Society described themselves as being of 'liberal views'. Cited Wyncoll (1985), p 95.

also held suffrage market stalls, concerts and garden parties. However, the Nottingham NUWSS branch records reveal that just over 100 members out of 300 lived in working-class areas of the city.[30]

However, a NUWSS meeting at East Circus Street Hall on 6 April was as well attended as that of the WSPU meeting on 7 May. What is interesting to note is that in Nottingham during this period there appears to be a close working relationship between the two groups and a level of reciprocity and shared comradeship. This was evident when Alice and Maud Dowson were invited by Emmeline Pankhurst to a WSPU meeting at the Albert Hall in London to welcome suffragettes released from prison on 20 March 1908, which they duly attended.[31]

There were no arrests in Nottingham in 1907-08, or none recorded that we have been able to discover; but at national level several prominent suffragettes had been imprisoned on the grounds of civil disobedience, leading to short prison sentences. Such 'disobedience' included disrupting meetings, refusing to move on and heckling Members of Parliament, and in 1907 Christabel Pankhurst stood trial for publishing a pamphlet that called on demonstrators to 'rush' the House of Commons.[32]

In June 1908, a large demonstration was organised by the Nottingham branch of the NUWSS along with other groups from across the East Midlands, and held at the Forest Recreation Ground. Further disappointment had followed the failure of a private member's bill in Parliament which had been introduced by the Liberal MP Henry Stanger, earlier in 1908. The demonstration on 11 June attracted 3,000 people and was addressed by Mrs Stanbury from the NUWSS executive, who had special responsibility for the Midlands. This was a peaceful occasion which passed off without incident. The event was recorded in the *Nottingham Guardian* of 12 June 1908. The Chairman for the meeting was noted as Mr C. L. Rothera, a local solicitor associated with the Liberal and Progressive Party and the Nottingham Men's League for Women's Suffrage. The newspaper reported that orderly proceedings had taken place and outlined Mrs Stanbury's address in which she advocated that

---

[30] Minutes of Nottingham and Nottinghamshire Branch, ref: DD 1334/11, Nottinghamshire Archives.
[31] Meynell, A. (1998), p 244.
[32] Holton, S. (2015) *Oxford National Biography*.

the suffragists were a just and common-sense movement, only asking for what was fair and right: their mission to help in creating a better, stronger, healthier country. The meeting closed with a vote on the resolution and the playing of the National Anthem.[33]

Two large, national Votes for Women demonstrations also took place in London that same year, the first on 14 June organised by the NUWSS attracted 10,000 supporters, including Nellie Dowson, secretary of the Nottingham branch, who travelled down to London with a party of 30 or more from the city. The suffragists marched through Central London to the Albert Hall in South Kensington, carrying banners and singing. On 21 June the WSPU held a rally in Hyde Park, London, after a march through the city. Billed as 'Suffrage Sunday', the event attracted 25,000 supporters. They were not the only suffrage society present: others, like the Fabian Society, also took part.[34]

On 30 June the WSPU gathered in Parliament Square, London, in protest at the indifference shown to these large demonstrations by women demanding the vote. This led to several arrests of suffragettes and marked the start of increased militancy by the WSPU. Present at this demonstration was a strong contingent of police officers and there were many reports of assault and intimidation of the women supporters by them. The action against the suffragettes led to two supporters taking a cab to 10 Downing Street where stones were thrown through the windows. The era of the 'window smasher' had begun (Hawksley 2013, p 152).

Another Nottingham demonstration organised by the WSPU was held on the Forest on 18 July 1908 and reported in the WSPU newspaper *Votes for Women* as follows:

> A great demonstration took place in Nottingham when the WSPU held a mass meeting with eight platforms, from which most of the leaders of the

---

[33] *The Nottingham Guardian*, 12.6.1908. The resolution read, "That this great meeting demands the vote for women on the same terms as it is, or may be given to men."
[34] Hawksley (2013), p 151.

movement spoke.[35] From twenty to thirty thousand people were present, the great majority of whom were attentive and friendly, and the resolution calling upon the Government to grant Votes for Women at once was passed by an overwhelming majority. At two of the platforms – those at which Mrs Pankhurst and Mrs Drummond spoke – a noisy gang of opponents clustered round, rendering hearing difficult, but the speakers proceeded in spite of the interruptions. At the other platforms complete order prevailed, and when some of the noisy gang from around Mrs Pankhurst's platform attempted to make a disturbance, they were promptly stopped by the audience.

The highest congratulations are due to Miss Nell Kenney and the splendid workers of the Nottingham Union, who are responsible for the success of the day.[36]

Included in *Votes for Women* is also an account provided by the *Nottingham Daily Express* which was surprisingly supportive, the reporter noting that the demonstration was remarkably successful, though placing the size of the crowd at between twelve to fifteen thousand people. Here is an extract:

There was little that was new in way of the arguments, but they were presented with such delightful freshness and vivacity that the crowds, where the roughs were absent, were never bored or restive. At every platform the same claim was emphasised, the speakers swaying to and fro in the heat of their arguments, and impressing the various points on the minds of their hearers with emphatic blows of hand on hand. The granting of the franchise to women, on the same terms, whatever they are, or may be; as enjoyed by men. That was the whole point of the argument. Presenting petitions and Parliamentary pirouetting, they urged had failed to bring women's enfranchisement into the arena of practical politics and therefore the only alternative was to enter upon a militant agenda.[37]

---

[35] The speakers included Emmeline Pankhurst, Emmeline Pethick Lawrence, Christabel Pankhurst, Gladice Keevil, Mrs Martel, Flora Drummond & Alice Hawkins from Leicester.
[36] *Votes for Women*, 18.7.1908.
[37] *Votes for Women*, 18.7.1908.

Arrests

In the early part of the next year events in London did have an impact on both of the main suffrage groups in Nottingham, when on 24 February 1909 Helen Kirkpatrick Watts, from the local WSPU group, was arrested outside the House of Commons with other suffragettes and sentenced to one month's imprisonment in Holloway Gaol. A copy of Helen's arrest papers can be found in the Nottinghamshire Archives, where the charge is described as "wilfully obstructing Police whilst in the due execution of their duty at Parliament Square."

Helen had joined the WSPU in 1907 after attending the meeting addressed by Christabel Pankhurst, when the women speakers had been appallingly treated. She was the daughter of Rev Alan Watts, vicar of Lenton. Just prior to this, in January 1909, Gladice Keevil, the WSPU Midlands Regional Organiser had been arrested for obstruction outside Winston Churchill's meeting at Victoria Hall, Nottingham, but was subsequently released. When news of Helen's imprisonment became known, messages of support flooded in, and on her release, she received an enthusiastic reception at Morley's Café on Wheeler Gate on 24 March 1909. Morley's Café was a frequent meeting place for Nottingham suffragettes during this period of time.

Ellen 'Nellie' Crocker replaced Rachel Barrett as the paid WSPU organiser in Nottingham in 1909 and remained in the city until 1912. She was also arrested in 1909 during a deputation to the House of Commons on 29 June and imprisoned with Mary Rawson, also from Nottingham. Nellie was a cousin of Emmeline Pethick Lawrence and gave her address as 8 East Circus Street.[38] Mary Rawson was also a WSPU organiser and she gave her address as 5 Carlton Street, Nottingham, that of the WSPU shop. Her release from prison was noted in the local press.[39]

The attention in the media to the increased militancy and arrests of the WSPU activists also benefitted the NUWSS and the local Nottingham branch held a mass meeting on 5 July 1909, buoyed up by public interest in securing votes for women. Margaret Ashton, Edward Carpenter and Eleanor Rathbone were all billed to speak in the Market-place and Nellie and Maud Dowson from the

---

[38] Crawford (2001), p 153.
[39] *Nottingham Evening Post,* 19.11.1910.

local branch were also present.[40] According to Alice Dowson's diary, the meeting ended in a "disgraceful riot" and "the ladies were badly hustled, Maud being struck."[41] At this meeting, anti-suffrage feeling was particularly evident and although the police had been informed of the event they had failed to attend and the meeting became unruly, even violent, with several speakers unable to continue. Nellie Dowson, in her capacity as Secretary of the NUWSS Branch, sent a letter of protest to the local press about the behaviour of the police, and wrote to Millicent Fawcett.

Anti-suffrage groups were also active in the city, holding two meetings in the same year. In January 1909 an anti-suffrage meeting at the Mechanics Hall was addressed by Mary Angela Dickens, the grand-daughter of Charles Dickens, who told the meeting that a woman's vote was irresponsible. The second meeting took place on 18 October 1909.[42]

On 27 July 1909 the Nottingham WSPU attempted to disrupt Sir James Yoxall's[43] meeting in the Albert Hall, Nottingham but were ejected, so they held a separate meeting in the Market-place where Helen Watts, Charlotte Marsh from the London WSPU, the Leicester organiser Laura Ainsworth and a Mrs Baines, also from Leicester, were all arrested but released without charge.[44]

Helen Watts was arrested again on 4 September 1909 in Leicester with Nellie Crocker, Mary Rawson and Alice Hawkins of Leicester WSPU at a meeting addressed by Winston Churchill, Home Secretary in Asquith's Liberal cabinet and opposed to female suffrage. The charge was 'disorderly conduct' simply for trying to enter the building where the meeting was taking place. Nellie, having gained entry, was charged with interrupting the meeting and was imprisoned with Helen and went on hunger strike but was released after four days. In Leicester Gaol, Helen also went on hunger strike and was threatened

---

[40] *Nottingham Evening Post*, 6.7.1909.
[41] Meynell (1998), p 246.
[42] *Nottingham Evening Post*, 19.10.1909.
[43] J. H. Yoxall, Liberal MP for the Nottingham West Constituency 1895-1918. He was also General Secretary of the National Union of Teachers.
[44] *Nottingham Evening Post*, 27.7.1909.

with force-feeding[45] but this didn't take place and she was released after five days.[46] In an address she gave at Morley's Café after her release, she remarked:

> "Votes for Women will not be won by drawing room chatter. It has got to be fought for in the market-places, and if we don't fight for it, no one else will.... The open-air meeting is a symbol *of the principles, the method, and the spirit of the most vigorous* movement towards Woman Suffrage in England today."[47]

On 6 September 1909 the Nottingham WSPU held a protest meeting in the Market-place to object to the arrests. Forcible feeding of suffragettes who deployed a hunger strike in protest when imprisoned was introduced by the Government in 1909 and was significantly commented upon by the local and national press. When Nellie Crocker, as WSPU organiser in Nottingham, suggested that force-feeding was not worthy of a civilised society, the *Nottingham Evening Post* editorial suggested, "Apparently window smashing and the wanton destruction of the property of unoffending persons are worthy of a civilised county."[48] Nottingham NUWSS were of the same mind as Nellie and several letters were published in the papers expressing condemnation.

During 1909 the NUWSS National Committee started to distance itself from the militancy of the WSPU. Arrests of local activists like Helen Watts and the WSPU organisers from Nottingham in Leicester and London were publicised in the local papers and had an impact on what appears to have been a strong working relationship between the two main suffrage groups in Nottingham. Letters between Nellie Dowson, leader of the city suffragists, and the national leader Millicent Fawcett reflect this development.

On 9 October 1909 Nellie wrote to express her concerns: the NUWSS branch in Nottingham, she felt, could not carry on the society in Nottingham without the people who would resign over a too strong condemnation of the WSPU.

---

[45] The first incidence of force-feeding took place at Winson Green Prison, Birmingham in 1909.
[46] Crawford, E. (2001), p 702.
[47] Cited by Crawford, E. (2001), p 701, from papers in Nottinghamshire Archives.
[48] *Nottingham Evening Post*, 6.9.1909.

Millicent Fawcett replied on 15 October, "I do not agree that the recent outbreak of almost criminal violence by the WSPU is caused by a few excitable members getting out of hand. It is premeditated and arranged and will get more violent. It is essential for the NUWSS to show they stand for peaceful persuasion."[49]

Mary Macarthur: the Nottingham campaign against sweated labour and Women's Suffrage

If there were, as suggested, close links between the two main women's suffrage groups in Nottingham, their association with women workers is much harder to determine. By 1890 there were a number of women's trade unions in the city as noted in the Minutes of the Nottingham Trades Council for that year. Nottingham Female Hosiery Workers Union was established in 1890 with 400 members on its books, and a branch for tailoresses that same year. In the lace trades, a Female Lace Workers Society had been in existence for some time, while a Lace Finishers Branch and a Female Cigar Workers Union had been formed in 1887.

In 1909 the National Federation of Women Workers (NFWW) directed a ten-day recruitment drive in Nottingham, holding dinner-hour meetings, outdoor meetings and a social event.[50] The drive to recruit women workers in the city stemmed in part from the legislative changes which had arisen from the Trade Boards Act of 1909. Trade Boards were established in paper box making, lace finishing, chain-making and ready-made and bespoke tailoring. These first Trade Boards, comprising appointed members, employers and workers' representatives, were tasked with setting minimum rates in the scheduled trades.[51] In order for minimum wages to be secured women needed to be recruited into trade unions and the Federation supplied two organisers to work in Nottingham with women lace workers, Mrs Young and Mrs Gosling, working alongside the secretary of the local Lace Finishers Branch, Miss

---

[49] Letters between Helena B. Dowson & Millicent Fawcett, October 1909. Women's Suffrage Collection, Manchester Central Library.
[50] Hunt (2014), pp 116-138.
[51] *ibid*

Peters. The difficulty in organising women workers in the lace trade lay in the arrangements by which the women secured their work as outworkers, hand-finishing the lace supplied by 'middle women' from the factories, which was extremely competitive. By 1906 there were around 14,000 women employed in the Nottingham lace trade and around half of these worked at home or in small workshops in the city and outlying villages.[52]

Mary Macarthur, General Secretary of the NFWW, travelled to Nottingham in1909 to support the recruitment drive and was photographed with a group of delegates, some of whom are thought to be suffragettes, attending a meeting in the city (see photo p 27). Macarthur was a supporter of adult suffrage but according to Angela V. John in the *Oxford Dictionary of National Biography*, she saw her primary commitment as providing protection for working-class women rather than concentrating on the voting rights of women.[53] It is most likely that the meeting that Macarthur was attending was the one organised by the Liberals at the Albert Hall on 27 July 1909 where the MP James Yoxall was speaking and members of the WSPU were ejected (see p 23).

1910 and the General Elections

There were two national elections during 1910, in January and December, a situation which had arisen when the House of Lords rejected the Peoples' Budget proposed by Lloyd George, eventually leading to a hung parliament and the Liberal MP Herbert Asquith forming a government with the support of the Irish Parliamentary Party, led by John Redmond. During Asquith's pre-election campaign he offered to find time in the new parliament to debate a women's suffrage bill.[54] Nottingham's NUWSS leadership, having remained active supporters of Liberalism in the city, staffed the polling booths to endorse the Liberal vote and also to gather signatures for petitions in support of women's enfranchisement. They were often greeted with hostility,[55] especially when the Unionist James Morrison beat the standing Liberal MP,

---

[52] *ibid*
[53] Hunt (2014), p 43.
[54] Annual Report of the Womens's Liberal Federation, 1909.
[55] Meynell (1998), pp 251-252.

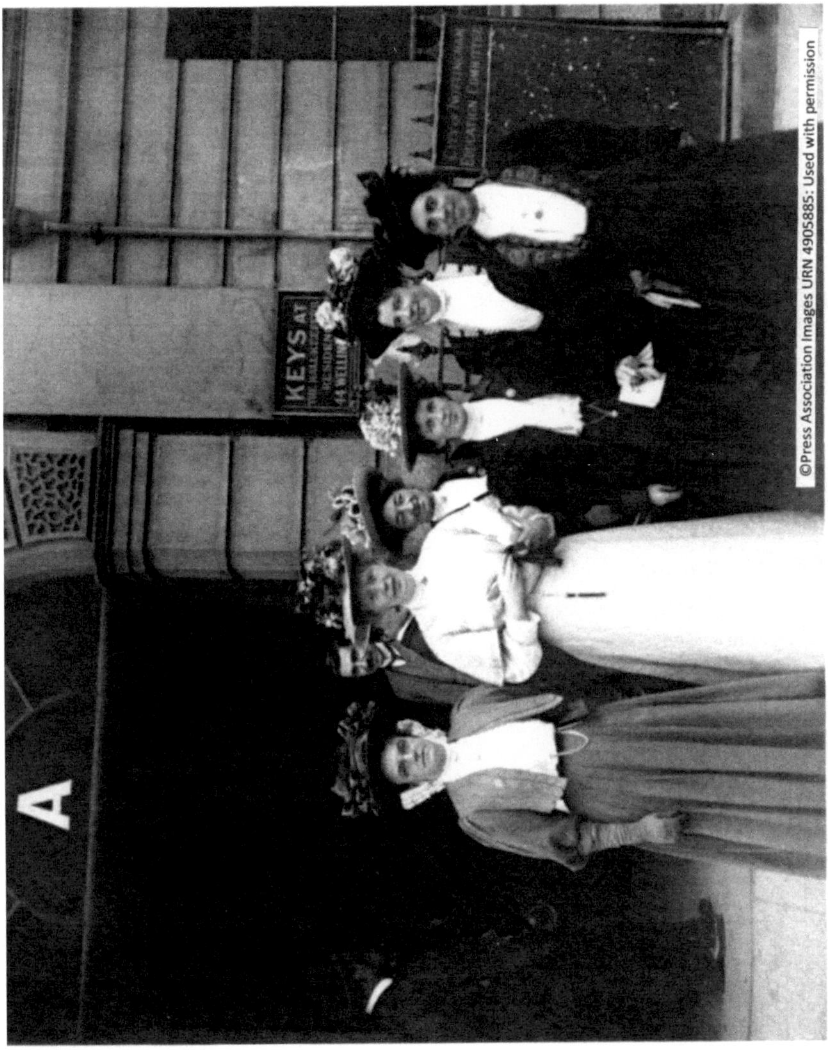
KEYS AT

Henry Cotton, in the first election in the Nottingham East constituency and again in the second election against the Liberal Dudley Stewart Smith. Nationally, there were big Liberal losses in both elections. The women's suffrage question inevitably came under scrutiny as it offered the potential to expand the electorate from the ranks of women, albeit limited to middle-class women who had for years shored up the Liberal Party. This led to the establishment of a conciliation committee for women's suffrage across four of the parliamentary political parties in February 1910.

The first Women's Franchise (Conciliation Bill) was drafted in 1910: the first reading of the bill took place in June of that year and it was passed by Parliament. Local NUWSS branches sent contingents of suffragists to London to join a demonstration in support of the second reading of the Conciliation Bill in July 1910 and the Nottingham branch sent thirty-two women including Maud, Nellie and Hilda Dowson.[56] All the suffrage groups were optimistic that the bill would prove to be successful and in anticipation of this, the NUWSS and the WSPU came together to form a united front, holding a grand rally in London on 23 July 1910 entitled 'From Prison to Citizenship'. The WSPU also agreed to suspend militancy.

Throughout 1910 the WSPU and the NUWSS continued to hold meetings in Nottingham attended by all the different suffrage groups in the city. In March 1910, Ethel Snowden *nee* Annakin addressed a NUWSS meeting at the Mechanics Institute. On 18 July, Adela Pankhurst and Dr Letitia Fairfield addressed a WSPU meeting in the Market-place; also present were Mrs Elsa Oswald, Miss Crook, and Dorothy Pethick who was now based in Leicester as an organiser.[57] Later that same month, on 25 July, the NUWSS organised a joint meeting with the Church League for Women's Suffrage (CLWS) in the Market-place in support of the Suffrage Bill which had been 'hung up' by the House of Commons. The meeting was addressed by CLWS founder, Rev Claude Hinscliffe and Frances Sterling from the NUWSS National Executive. In his address, Hinscliffe said:

> The movement was an absolutely moral one. It was the duty of everyone calling himself a Christian to stand by those whose lot was not cast in

---

[56] *Ibid*, p 253.
[57] *Nottingham Evening Post*, 19.7.1910.

pleasant places. No woman, whether in the castle or the cottage, could disregard the question of the suffrage.[58]

The intention of the Church League, which was established in 1909, was to join together on a non-party basis suffragists of every shade of opinion who were church - or chapel - people, to secure for women the vote in Church and State. Hinscliffe's wife Gertrude had been involved in social work in Nottingham and he attributed the setting-up of the League to their inspirational and mutually-supportive union. The Church League never spoke out against the tactics of the WSPU. In 1913 the League became the United Religious League and then, in 1917, changed its name again to the League of the Church Militant, campaigning for equality between men and women and for the ordination of women.[59] The Church League published a book by Ursula Roberts about the suffrage movement, *The Cause of Purity and Women's Suffrage* (1912). Roberts (1887-1971), a well-published author, became a key member of the Movement for the Ordination of Women; she was also Hon. Treasurer and Press Secretary of the East Midlands Federation of the NUWSS.

In September 1910 Lady Constance Lytton addressed WSPU and NUWSS members at a meeting held in Calvert's Café, Long Row, about her experiences of imprisonment and force-feeding.

In November 1910 the progress of the Conciliation Bill faltered when, with an impending second General Election in December, the Government stalled the introduction of the Bill into Parliamentary business on the basis that there was no time. In response to Asquith's refusal to allow facility time for the Women's Suffrage Bill, the NUWSS and the WSPU joined forces to protest this turn of events.

Elizabeth Garrett Anderson (NUWSS supporter and sister of Millicent Fawcett) and Emmeline Pankhurst from the WSPU led a deputation of women in a march to the House of Commons on 18 November. The day began at Caxton Hall in Westminster which the WSPU frequently used for meetings, but this time it also included members of the NUWSS. The intention was to

---

[58] *Nottingham Evening Post*, 26.7.1910.
[59] Records of the League of the Church Militant, The Women's Library, LSE. Also: Austin, M. (2012*) 'Like a Swift Hurricane': People, Clergy and Class in a Midlands Diocese*, 1914-1919. Chesterfield: Merton Priory Press.

meet with Prime Minister Asquith and confront him. When the demonstration moved off, the women were met by a large contingent of police officers who mobbed them, kicking, pinching and punching and using sexual violence against them.[60] The event was to become known as 'Black Friday' and 115 women and four men were arrested, but later released. The net effect was to "swing public opinion more firmly in support of the suffrage movement" (Hawksley 2013, p 170). Several WSPU members from Nottingham and Leicester were amongst those arrested: Lillian Hickling,[61] Nellie Crocker, Muriel Wallis and Elsie Hall.

Following Black Friday, on 22 November members of the WSPU targeted Asquith himself and a 400-strong mob of suffragettes stormed Downing Street, taking the police by surprise at the anger of the women. This time there were 150 arrests and Churchill, then Home Secretary, showed no leniency and all were imprisoned.

In Nottingham the NUWSS were clearly disappointed with Asquith and the Liberal Government. In her diary, Alice Dowson commented on the events following Black Friday:

> "[It was] a critical day for suffragists at Westminster: this government tries to play with them... I was furious to hear how Mr Asquith has again disappointed us with his false and empty promises! & the Militants made a great riot in Westminster yesterday. Quite justified I think!"[62]

The NUWSS particularly benefitted from the renewed press coverage and public support for women's suffrage, evident in the increase in national membership to 21,571, making it the largest suffrage group. They proclaimed, nonetheless, that their approach would remain constitutional, the NUWSS leaders reproaching the WSPU for breaking the truce in respect of the use of militant tactics, when there was still life in the Conciliation Bill.

---

[60] Henry Brailsford and Dr Jessie Murray interviewed the women and wrote a report about the abuse, which is in the British Library in London.
[61] Lillian Maud Hickling (1885-1975). In 1911 she lived at Sutherland Lodge, Lucknow Drive, Mapperley Park. She is named on the Suffragette Roll of Honour.
[62] Meynell (1998), p 254.

In 1910, the NUWSS was reorganised and Federations were created comprised of local affiliated societies, some 200 branches in total. In Nottinghamshire, the smaller towns like Hucknall and Mansfield established their own NUWSS branches. In 1913 the NUWSS Midlands Federation divided into two separate Federations: Midlands East and Midlands West.

The second General Election drew 1910 to a close; in her diary, Alice Dowson summed up the mood of many suffrage activists:

> "This year (1911) opens with a lately-elected Parliament, the 2nd in one year, the result being nearly the same as before. Mr Asquith & the Liberals remain in power, but the Irish hold the balance. Suffrage I fear stands a poor chance; Nellie, Hilda and Maud are indefatigable."[63]

The Suffragette Census Boycott in Nottingham, 1911

In April 1911 a Census boycott was introduced as a new tactic by suffragettes and suffragists who reasoned that if the Government would not comply with, or even listen to, their demands, then they would not comply with the Government's data-gathering exercise. Some women absented themselves completely and did not fill in the census form, while others spoiled their forms by writing slogans such as "No vote, no census" on them.

The Census had been introduced in 1801 as a means of gaining information about the population in order to plan policy and public spending, but it was mainly statistical until 1851 when more personal data began to be required about familial relationships, place of birth etc. The UK Census is taken every 10 years, and becomes available as a matter of public record 101 years later and in 2011 the reasons for the above-mentioned boycott became clear. The 1911 Census required much more personal detail than the few basic facts which had been gathered previously, because the Liberal Government wanted to introduce reforms to improve housing, health and welfare for vulnerable members of society, including reducing infant mortality. For the first time, women were required to state how many live children they had given birth to,

---

[63] *ibid* p 254: reference to Irish Unionist MPs.

how many of those children were still alive and how many had died (Liddington, 2014); (Bounds, 2014).

In their wisdom, however, the Government officers responsible for the 1911 Census decreed that only the Heads of Household, i.e. *enfranchised men*, were eligible to complete the forms, which would entail asking highly personal, intrusive and potentially distressing questions of the women in their household about childbirth. The Civil Servants did not seem to consider how deeply women would feel about having to defer to the men in the household about these sensitive issues, let alone being denied the opportunity to record their own details in their own voice.

Allied to this simmering resentment and stoked by the 'killing' of the two Conciliation Bills on women's suffrage, was the growing movement of non-compliance and passive resistance, represented by the Women's Freedom League (WFL)[64] and the Women's Tax Resistance League (WTRL). The former had decided on the tactic of non-cooperation with the Government until women were granted the vote; whilst the latter felt that demanding Census information about women without those women being able to determine how the information was used, equated to demanding equal taxes from women without them being able to say how their taxes should be spent (Bounds, 2014).

With Census night set for Sunday 2 April, women's campaigning groups began actively preparing for the boycott in February 1911, although the idea had first been suggested as early as June 1910 by Edith How-Martin, when the intrusive nature of the additional questions was not even known. How-Martin, a mathematics lecturer and head of the WFL Political and Militant Department, reasoned that a non-militant boycott would be more likely to impress and influence both Parliament and the public.

The WPSU joined forces with the WFL to produce and disseminate information through their meetings and newspapers about methods of non-compliance and any potential penalties participants might face. A slogan evolved, which encapsulated the principle of the boycott: 'If women don't

---

[64] The WFL was a break away group from the WSPU formed in 1907. We have not so far found any activity in Nottingham from this group.

count, don't count women' – and two forms of action were identified: resistance and evasion.

Resistance required the householder to withhold information by refusing to complete the form and giving their reason – typically by writing 'No Vote, No Census' instead. It was, and still is, an offence to refuse to complete the form, and householders could be fined £5 or even imprisoned if they refused to pay, so this measure was not without consequences. Evasion, on the other hand, was not illegal. It merely entailed an individual being away from home on Census night so that their details could not be recorded. Campaigning groups suggested several means to achieve this: one was by travelling all night, while another was to attend a social event in a public building. In her 2014 book, *Vanishing for the Vote*, Jill Liddington mentions the Aldwych Skating Rink on the Strand in London, where 570 men and women were accommodated; likewise, the Gardenia Restaurant in Covent Garden, where 230 men and women were involved. Yet another tactic was to stay overnight with someone who would be willing to say they did not know who was resident in their house at the time of the Census (Bounds, 2014). Liddington has catalogued some of the mass evasions involving both men and women at the homes of suffrage campaigners throughout England, some accommodating as few as six, one accommodating as many as 208.

However, the suffrage movement was divided over the issue of the Census boycott. One side of the argument was that providing the Government with the more detailed and more accurate information was desirable because the reforms arising from it would be of great benefit to women. The other side felt that it was wrong of the Government to ask for such information about women whilst denying them citizenship. Another consideration was that the boycott needed to be wide-spread with mass evasion or resistance if it was to have any meaningful impact and gain the publicity it wanted (Bounds, 2014). The WFL and the WSPU were dismayed that the largest women's suffrage organisation, the NUWSS, did not support these tactics.

Because the NUWSS was pledged to non-militant, constitutional campaigning for the vote, it had been hoped, even anticipated, that evasion and resistance would appeal to its members; but it decided against supporting the measure at its AGM in January 1911 (Bounds, 2014). This division was noted by the national newspapers and, naturally, some used it to ridicule and undermine the cause, while *The Manchester Guardian*, as it was then known, although supporting the cause, urged women not to participate in the boycott but to provide the information required, to bring about reform.

So, women, and men too, had much to consider when deciding whether (or not) to participate in the Census boycott. Joy Bounds (2014) explains that it was an unprecedented act of civil disobedience; therefore the consequences could not be predicted. Indeed, not even the enumerators were sure of what they should do in such an event. She goes on to say that it would have been particularly difficult for women in smaller communities where everyone would have known everyone else, so no woman would have undertaken this action lightly.

There are six recorded Nottingham evaders identified to date:

Catherine Mary (May) Burgis
Muriel Wallis
Ellen (Nellie) Crocker, WSPU organiser in Nottingham
Sarah Hutchinson[65]
Leonora Shaw – a member of the CLWS
Miss Greenhall

Additionally, there were at least two Nottingham suffragists who joined the boycott as resisters: Alice Watts, sister of Helen Watts, at home at Lenton Vicarage (now Unity House), recorded her occupation as 'Secretary, Suffragist Society'.[66] And Kate Eleanor Gillick who lived in Carrington also took part in the boycott, though she does not appear to have participated in suffrage demonstrations.[67] Other emerging examples seem to indicate that some women who were not members of the suffrage societies took this opportunity to express their support.

It is estimated that thousands of women may be missing from the 1911 Census, but exact numbers will never be known. If you decide to research

---

[65] The Friends' League for Women's Suffrage was set up in Nottingham by Sarah Hutchinson of 5 Cavendish Crescent, The Park. The aim of the FLWS was "To secure for women the Parliamentary Franchise on the same terms as it is or may be granted to men" (Crawford, p 233).
[66] Liddington (2014), pp 333-335.
[67] *Nottingham Evening Post,* 22.7.201 in *Bygones* supplement, 'Votes for Women'.

your family history and one or several of your female ancestors disappeared on Census night 1911, they may have been Census evaders.

Direct Action

By mid-June 1911, the successful second reading of a new Conciliation Bill for women's suffrage in May had raised the hopes of the suffrage movement once again, and a 40,000 strong 'Women's Coronation Procession' took place on 17 June 1911 in London. The event passed peacefully and brought together many different suffrage societies. Alice Dowson refers to this in her diary as "a splendid occasion" with one hundred Nottingham NUWSS supporters in the contingent.

In November, however, the Asquith Government Reform Bill intended to extend suffrage to all men, dismayed and infuriated suffrage campaigners in equal measure despite, or probably because of, Asquith's casually patronising suggestion that "suffragists might, if they wished, attach an amendment for women."[68] It can be argued, then, that the escalation of the women's suffrage campaign to acts of violent protest was a direct result of Asquith's action. Seen as a betrayal of the women's suffrage cause, it motivated many mainly WSPU members to adopt more radical means of making their voices heard. Campaigns of window smashing, post box tampering and even arson were stepped up, not only in London but across the country, especially in the Northern industrial centres like Leeds, Sheffield, Doncaster and York. Involved in the first wave of large-scale window smashing in London in 1912 was the Nottingham WSPU organizer, Nellie Crocker, and another WSPU member, Gladys Roberts, who was working as co-organiser with Crocker. An article in the *Nottingham Evening Post* (8.6.12) reported Nellie's and Gladys's return home after the London action, having spent 1st March - 4th June in Holloway prison - three months in total.

Due to the absence of written records for the Nottingham Branch, it has been difficult to gauge the support for the WSPU at this period, but most of the evidence suggests that the organisation had become somewhat dissipated in the city by 1912, with the paid organisers, when present, instigating any

---

[68] Liddington, J. (2014), pp 206-207.

collective action, particularly involving militancy which was to escalate further in 1913 and 1914. However, in March 1912, a local WSPU member, using the alias 'Annie Baker' was arrested in London for smashing shop windows and sent to prison. Her true identity was Edith Annie Lees (read more on page 62). Helen Watts, despite her initial involvement, had relocated to Bath by 1912 and commenced nursing training at the Royal National Hospital there. May Burgis, who had been the Honorary Secretary in Nottingham from 1907 and active in the 1911 Census boycott, stepped down; and Nellie Crocker, WSPU organiser 1909-1912, also disappears from the record at this point when her aunt and uncle, Emmeline and Frederick Pethick Lawrence, key players and financial backers for the National Organisation, left the WSPU in 1912.[69] They had argued for the need to return to building and demonstrating popular support for women's enfranchisement. Emmeline's sister, Dorothy Pethick, the WSPU organiser in Leicester, also left the organisation in 1912.

Several lower-key meetings were organised by the WSPU during 1912, mainly taking place in smaller venues such as school rooms. With Nellie Crocker in Holloway, Sylvia Pankhurst came to the city when a by-election was called in the East Nottingham constituency,[70] followed by her mother, Emmeline Pankhurst, in June for the Ilkeston by-election. 1912 also witnessed some important changes in the way the NUWSS approached their campaign, especially after Asquith's announcement of a Manhood Suffrage Bill and the demise of the Third Conciliation Bill. The NUWSS abandoned the strategy of seeking Government support for Private Member's Bills and started to press instead for a Government measure that might include women. This led to active support for Labour Party candidates after its 1912 Annual Conference declared support for women's suffrage. An NUWSS election fighting fund was established[71] and several democratic measures were put in place to link the NUWSS more closely with grass-root organisations fighting for universal suffrage. So, for example, greater co-operation was proposed with Church groups, the Trade Unions and the Women's Co-operative Guild. The NUWSS also introduced a 'Friends of Women's Suffrage Scheme' whereby working women could pledge their support without payment.

---

[69] Holton, S. (2015), *Oxford Dictionary of National Biography*.
[70] The Conservative Party won the seat.
[71] The Election Fighting Fund or EFF was to support Labour candidates in three-cornered contests as a means of endangering Government-held seats.

This interesting change of tactics was not mirrored in Nottingham, where the campaign against sweated labour of the lace outworkers continued but appears to have had little documented support from either the NUWSS or WSPU in the city or from the public. In 1911 the National Federation of Women Workers had begun an extensive organisation of Nottingham outworkers, many of whom were earning no more than one shilling and three pence per day.[72] The NFWW also established an office at 13 George Street with a Miss Peters, Kathleen Mollison and Esther Young as union organisers.[73] A lock-out of lace workers took place in 1911 when they refused to contract out of the Trades Board rate for the first six months and the Nottingham Trades Council gave financial support; consequently Federation membership increased. However, by 1912 it was noted that there was significant victimisation of Federation members and payments well below the minimum wage continued to be paid. One can only deduce that by 1912, the different movements to improve women's lives in the city were somewhat fragmented.

In late 1912 Charlotte Marsh, a key WSPU figure and a militant suffragette, replaced Nellie Crocker as organiser in Nottingham. Charlotte had a long history of militancy and had been imprisoned many times. She was often referred to in the Nottingham press, indicating that she was well known to the authorities. In February 1912 the *Nottingham Daily Express* had interviewed her regarding acts of militancy.

The Nottingham WSPU meanwhile continued with a range of protests in both city and county during 1913 as the following overview outlines:

> * 7 February - Pillar boxes attacked in Nottingham. Black fluid poured into post boxes across the city.[74] 'Votes for Women' stickers were found at each incident and the press took every opportunity to condemn the protesters' actions as reckless and liable to alienate the public's sympathies.
> * 19th February - Police foiled planned attack on links at Bulwell Golf Club.
> * 20th February - Pillar boxes attacked in Mansfield.

---

[72] *Sunday Chronicle*, 17.11.1909.
[73] Hunt (2014), *The National Federation of Women Workers*, p 58.
[74] *Nottingham Evening Post*, 7.2.1913.

* 24th February - Pillar boxes attacked with phosphorus in Beeston.
* 25th February - WSPU interrupt Sir James Yoxall's meeting in Stanley Street School, Nottingham; seven women forcibly ejected.
* 17th April - More pillar boxes attacked in Nottingham.
* 26th April - Attempt to disrupt meeting of Mr Acland, MP[75] in Nottingham's Albert Hall.

The tactic of interrupting and openly castigating Liberal MPs by the WSPU was frequently utilised, as demonstrated in this report in the *Hucknall Dispatch* of a meeting held at the Baptist School Room, Station Street, Carlton on 10 November 1913, where the Liberal Member, Mr Leif Jones, a supporter of women's suffrage, was speaking:

> Mr Jones had only uttered a few introductory sentences about their opponents getting ready for a general election – preparations against which he had no complaints to make – when a suffragist stood up and asked why the Government continued to deny votes to women, who were imprisoned and tortured under the 'Cat and Mouse' Act. Mr Jones replied that for himself he was a supporter of votes for women, but he contended that the methods of certain women jeopardised their chances of getting the vote. The lady again made a remark as to why the Government did not act.

Further interruptions ensued:

> However, the lady would not be quieted and such remarks as "Shut up, old bird, or you will be turned out," and "Chuck her through the window" came from masculine throats. Pleading for a hearing, Mr Jones said they had not yet a verdict from the country.
> "It is time you had," quoth the suffragist... one man came from the back of the hall to assist in the operation of ejecting the lady, who was not handled 'with care,' inasmuch as men seized her arms and commenced to use force. The suffragist was soon subdued, and was led away in comparative quietness. Another woman immediately took her place and interjected, and then a third and they too were grabbed by several men and hurried from the hall.

---

[75] Acland was Under Secretary for Foreign Affairs

Also reported in the same edition was the following note:

> On 20 November 1913 at Long Eaton, at the opening of the new Labour Hall, 20 suffragettes were ejected in a similar fashion.

The WSPU national strategy was to continue with militant tactics which became increasingly more complex and the Government responded with more repressive measures, including the introduction of the 'Cat and Mouse Act' of 1913[76] in March. This act allowed the police and prison wardens to release suffragette hunger strikers in poor health on licence, to be re-arrested when they recovered. A public outcry over this approach once again galvanised the WSPU in Nottingham where there was a spate of protest initiatives. On 12 March 1913, at a WSPU meeting addressed by Annie Kenney at Circus Street Hall, women were attacked by gangs of men and the Nottingham Watch Committee received a claim for damages. This was rejected by the Chief Constable who stated that all halls must take responsibility for damages, a measure which resulted in reluctance to let out meeting spaces for suffragette meetings in Nottingham.

Various retaliatory actions were taken against the suffragettes: for example, the smashing of windows at the WSPU offices on Bridlesmith Gate, apparently a protest at suffragettes trying to break up a meeting in the city where the Liberal MP and Under-Secretary of State, F.D. Acland, declared that militancy was "pure insanity." Local newspapers reported that responses to, and activities of, the suffragettes were causing considerable trouble to the Police of the Nottingham and District Watch, who were taking additional measures, including a watch on Nottingham Castle. Several demonstrations took place in Nottingham to protest the Cat and Mouse Act during this period of renewed activity, but there were no arrests made.

The WSPU campaign continued apace: on 12 May 1913, the spectacular burning down of Nottingham Boat Club was watched by an eager crowd from the safety of Trent Bridge. Investigations soon made it clear that the fire had been the result of arson rather than an accident and it can be speculated that the target had been selected as a bastion of male attitudes, following the failure of yet another Parliamentary attempt to extend voting rights to women.

---

[76] The Prisoners (Temporary Discharge for Ill Health) Act 1913 was the formal title.

Described as "the latest outrage of militant suffragists" by the *Nottingham Evening Post*, a group of women had set fire to the new Britannia Boat House on the River Trent.[77] Approximately £2,000 worth of damage was done, and the suffragettes wrote: "Be thankful that we haven't gone further; if we had been men, life would have been taken ages ago."[78] Such was the pity other men felt for the poor boaters that various clubs in the region offered to lend them boats, and proffered great sympathy.

On 26 July 1913 a demonstration was held in the Market-place with four platforms of speakers, a large contingent of policemen and, according to the *Nottingham Daily Express*, a crowd of 10,000. There was also some response from the Nottingham trade unions, specifically the Nottingham branch of the National Union of Railwaymen, who called on the Government to stop the forcible feeding of suffragettes and grant adult suffrage. On 12 December 1913 Emmeline Pankhurst returned to the city to speak at the Corn Exchange where it was advertised as a women-only event – with the proviso that men *could* be admitted on the guarantee of a member of the WSPU![79]

The Suffrage Movement in the County

Suffragist and suffragette activity was not confined to the city of Nottingham. Smaller branches, mainly affiliated to the NUWSS, existed in the surrounding towns and villages, ready and willing to support demonstrations and recruit members. Inevitably, records of these groups are patchy and as this edition goes to press we regret that we have been unable to find much information about some places: for example, we know that in Newark a branch of the National Society for Women's Suffrage existed as early as 1872 and an NUWSS branch was established in 1910. However, no other information has yet become available.

.

---

[77] *Nottingham Evening Post*, 12.5.2013.
[78] *Nottingham Evening Post*, 17.5.1913.
[79] *Nottingham Evening Post*, 2.12.1913.

Mansfield

Mansfield Women's Suffrage Society was formed in October 1893[80] when Millicent Fawcett came to address the inaugural meeting. She would return several times to Mansfield over the years. In 1898 the Mansfield Women's Liberal Association also affiliated to the NUWSS to support the suffrage cause. The President was Louisa Wright (1849-1916), who was born into a Quaker family near Ely, Cambridgeshire. In the 1900s she was living at 87 West Hill Drive in Mansfield. A veteran campaigner, she remained President until her death in 1916, and she was not replaced. The Honorary Secretary was another Quaker, Emily Manners *nee* Barringer (1857-1934), who also represented Mansfield on the National Executive of the NUWSS. Her sister, Louisa Maria Barringer, was involved as a Committee member. In 1901 Emily was elected as a Poor Law Guardian and would become one of the first female Justices of the Peace in the town.

In 1900 Millicent Fawcett addressed a public meeting at Mansfield Town Hall, where there was a small attendance, but numbers gradually increased. In 1902 the *Mansfield Advertiser* reported on an assembly of the Mansfield WSS to hear Mrs C. Mallett of London speak on 'The Vote, Women's Heritage and Protection.'[81] Clementina Black from the Women's Industrial Council addressed a meeting on 27 November 1907 at the Old Meeting House: in attendance were representatives from the Women's Liberal Association and the Women's Total Abstinence Union who pledged their support for women's suffrage[82] - Mansfield NUWSS seems to have had a knack for bringing other organizations on board. In October 1908 the local Liberal MP, A.B. Markham and his wife addressed a meeting on the issue of employment and women's suffrage. Mrs Markham said that she was very much in favour of the suffrage but she was still more of a Liberal, despite the Liberals doing themselves a great deal of harm (a reference to the failure of the Liberal Government to implement the suffrage for women).[83]

---

[80] Crawford, E. (2001), p 761.
[81] *Mansfield Advertiser*, 3.10.1902.
[82] *Nottingham Journal*, 27.11.1907.
[83] *Nottingham Journal* 27.10.1908.

Open-air meetings, bazaars, garden parties and drawing-room meetings fill the Minute Books[84] and reveal the names of nearly eighty local women who were involved over the years. A Junior Suffrage Society was formed by a Miss Penlow in 1911, "for educating the younger generation on the suffrage question" (Minutes, 11.3.11). In 1913 members were fund-raising for the Suffrage Pilgrimage which was scheduled to pass through Mansfield in July; it attracted much attention in the press and carried the NUWSS message of non-militant engagement to many towns and villages in the area (see 'Women on the Move' below).

During WW1, when suffrage activity was suspended for the duration, the Society joined forces with groups like the Women's Co-operative Guild and the Municipal Distress Committee and also supported a Mother and Baby Welcome Group, a Clothing Committee, Women's Patrols in Mansfield, and aid for Russian refugees.

On 8 February 1918 the Committee unanimously adopted the following resolution: "That this Committee Meeting of the NUWSS Mansfield Branch desires to record its profound satisfaction that after fifty years of ceaseless agitation the political emancipation of women has at last been achieved and that the measure has now been placed on the Statute Book (the Representation of the People Bill Feb 6 1918) by which… women are enfranchised."

Mansfield NUWSS disbanded on 5 March 1919.

Southwell

A branch of the NUWSS was established in Southwell in 1910, prompted by Mrs Mary Hoskyns, wife of Bishop Edwyn Hoskyns,[85] who declared that she had for some years been interested in the objects of the Society and moved a resolution "that the vote should be granted to women on the same terms as men." Nellie Dowson gave an address and Mrs Hoskyns, Mrs W. H. Blandy, and Mrs Handford were duly elected to the Committee, Miss V. Smith to be Secretary.[86]

---

[84] Nottinghamshire Archives ref: DD 1354/70 & 72
[85] The Hoskyns, like the Riddings, were well-known supporters of women's suffrage
[86] *Nottingham Evening Post,* 23.4.1910.

The Southwell Branch seems to have been largely supported by the clergy and their families. For example, the Honorary Secretary, Miss Valentia Smith, of Vicar's Court, was a daughter of the late vicar of Halam; and the vicar of Farnsfield, Rev Robert McKee, presided over a public meeting of mainly women and young people on 5 April 1913 in support of the NUWSS (Southwell Branch). The speaker, Miss Norma Smith, "expressed great satisfaction at having the vicar in the chair to support the cause."[87]

On 9 July 1913 the Southwell Branch welcomed the Suffrage Pilgrimage on its way to Newark (see below).

Hucknall

Nellie Dowson held a suffrage meeting in Hucknall in 1910 but it was 1913 before a branch of the NUWSS was formed. According to the local newspaper, *The Dispatch*,[88] Nellie, "an indefatigable worker on behalf of women," had given "a rousing address" at Hucknall Women's Adult School the previous week, and this seems to have done the trick. But in the Letters column in the same issue, 'Socialist' began a campaign of anti-suffrage opinion. He -or she- opined:

> "If votes are granted to any woman now, it will be a distinct triumph for the militant suffragists, and we may as well close Parliament and let the Pankhursts act as supreme autocrats. Now is the time to resist them however drastic the measures that society may be compelled to take against them in its own defence."

In spite of opposition from some quarters, the newly-formed NUWSS Branch moved into premises above a tea shop on High Street (nos. 8-10) and Sarah B. Merrick of The Knoll, Beardall Street, became Secretary. The Society was a member of the Midland (East) Federation.

---

[87] *Nottingham Evening Post,* 7.4.1913
[88] *The Dispatch,* 6.3.1913

Letters to *The Dispatch* became progressively nastier: for example, in response to the incident at Carlton Baptist School Room, referred to on page 38, 'Uncle Tom' wrote:

> "Dear Sir – the Suffragettes got roughly treated on Monday night, so probably in future they will 'Leif' Jones alone. If not, I suggest the following remedy; six strokes with the birch rod, the punishment to be administered by a stalwart policeman or prison warder who has recently been crossed in love."[89]

Hucknall NUWSS continued until at least April 1914 when a speaker, Mrs Nesbitt, wife of a Sutton-in-Ashfield doctor, criticized the Liberal Party for neglecting to accord justice to women.[90]

See pages 64-65 for more about Sarah Merrick.

Retford

For a short period the town had an active WSPU branch and shop,[91] probably because the Nottingham WSPU organizer, Nellie Crocker (1872-1962), spent some time there during a by-election in 1910. In her memoirs, Crocker mentions that she hired a car to take her to Retford and engaged a driver. At a large open-air meeting in the town the atmosphere quickly turned hostile, and she relates how she and her co-worker, Gladys Roberts, were rescued by the landlord of a local hotel.[92]

Marion Holmes *nee* Milner (1867-1943), a biographer and playwright who grew up in Retford, went on to become an active suffragette and also, in later life, a notable Christian feminist. Her unpublished autobiography was placed in the Museum of London after her death.

---

[89] *The Dispatch*, 13.11.1913.
[90] *Nottingham Evening Post*, 1.4.1914.
[91] Located on St John Street, Retford.
[92] Girton College, Cambridge, Archives ref: GC RF8/1/4/1.

Women on the move

The summer of 1913 witnessed the Women's Suffrage Pilgrimage: eight cohorts of NUWSS members walked or cycled from various points around Britain, converging eventually in Hyde Park for a major rally. This was at the height of the Edwardian women's suffrage campaign with the NUWSS claiming nearly 100,000 members. The idea for the Pilgrimage was suggested by Katherine Harley (1855-1917),[93] a senior figure in the NUWSS, as a means to demonstrate to Parliament how many women wanted the vote and to emphasize that the NUWSS was essentially a non-militant organisation. The Newcastle to London route led by Miss I. Beaver was joined by members of the Nottingham suffragists as part of the East Midland, North, East and West Ridings and the Eastern Counties Federations of the NUWSS.

At each small town and village on the route the marchers were met by local supporters and public meetings were held. The media reported their progress[94] so, for example, on 8 July the Great North Road contingent left Chesterfield, holding five meetings before arriving at the village of Pleasley, near Mansfield. At Pleasley Hill the marchers were met by their leader Millicent Fawcett who addressed a meeting in the vicarage grounds; also present were Lady Madeline Onslow,[95] Louisa Wright and Mrs Manners, activists from the Mansfield branch. The contingent then set off to the music of the Pleasley Colliery Band, the route lined with hundreds of people as the marchers approached Mansfield for the main meeting in the Market Place where they encountered scenes of hostility and rowdyism. Emily Manners told the crowd:

> "We desire to improve the conditions of women socially, industrially… and we do not think this great object can be attained by smashing windows, blowing up houses and actions of that kind."[96]

From Mansfield, the Pilgrimage set off next day for Southwell and from there to Newark on 11 July, where a crowd of between 3,000 to 4,000 people was recorded. An official complaint was later made to the Watch Committee *via*

---

[93] Crawford (2001), p 27.
[94] Nottinghamshire Archives, ref: DD 1334/11.
[95] Madeline Onslow (1851-1926) was an Australian who appears to have resided in Derby during this period.
[96] Report in NUWSS paper, *The Common Cause*, n/d.

the Home Office about the amount of drunkenness and bad language encountered at Newark.[97] The women then headed for Grantham, holding a meeting at the village of Long Bennington *en route*.[98]

The Pilgrimage ended in London in Hyde Park on Saturday 26 July and a *Lincoln* newspaper[99] of 28 July1913 recorded the event as follows:

> Nottingham and other centres in the East Midlands contributed their quota to the great assemblage of non-militant suffragists in Hyde Park on Saturday ... at which speeches were delivered from 20 platforms to an audience of 30,000 or 40,000 people. A carriage was reserved on the 8.25 train from Nottingham on Saturday to carry up to London enthusiastic suffragists from Nottingham, Mansfield and the neighbourhood, and the societies at Leicester, Grantham, Ilkeston, Kettering, Oundle, Derby and Lincoln also sent contingents.
>
> The banner of the East Midland Federation attracted much attention by its gorgeous colouring and its message of undying determination[100]: and Nottingham's banner with its representation of the Castle was eagerly recognised by the crowds, and shouts such as "Good old Nottingham," "Good old lace curtains" and the like were heard all along the route.
>
> On the platform reserved for the East Midland Federation Miss Norma Smith (Derby)[101] took the chair and the speakers were Mrs Stanbury (NUWSS Executive with responsibility for the East Midlands), Mr Cholmely of the Men's League for Women's Suffrage and Mrs W. E. [Nellie] Dowson whose untiring work for women's suffrage is known to all Nottingham people.

Near this platform were seen Lady Yoxall[102] and Mrs Manners of Mansfield.

The Pilgrimage raised £8,000 for the NUWSS campaign in England and was viewed as being a significant undertaking by the constitutional campaign for

---

[97] *Lincolnshire Chronicle*, 26.8.1913.
[98] *Grantham Journal*, 12 .7.1913.
[99] The cutting on file is incomplete and the source has not been identified.
[100] From the evidence of a b & w photo, the East Midland banner depicted a phoenix within a large sun-burst: Nottinghamshire Archives, ref: DD 1354/70/ix.
[101] Norma Smith was one of the organisers of the Great North Road route.
[102] Lady Yoxall was the wife of J. H. Yoxall, MP for Nottingham West from1895.

suffrage. As Elizabeth Crawford notes, "Involvement in the Pilgrimage represented to some members of the constitutional society an experience as unusual and memorable as imprisonment was to members of the WSPU" (2001, p 550).

More disruption

Meanwhile, the WSPU in Nottingham was protesting about the Cat and Mouse Act and advertised a demonstration in Nottingham Market-place with four platforms of speakers from London,[103] to protest against the Act and to demand votes for women on the weekend before the NUWSS Pilgrimage ended on Monday 28th July. A number of letters to the Nottingham press condemning the Act preceded the event, including two from Charles L. Rothera of Forest Grove, the City Coroner, Deputy Mayor, local solicitor and a staunch member of the Liberal party.[104]

During this period relatively peaceful, but equally disruptive, measures were employed in churches by the WSPU. On 16 November 1913, at St Mary's Church in the Lace Market, several women started to chant along with the curate during the prayers, but using their own words to demand the vote. Although the police were sent for, there were no further interruptions and the women left at the end of the service.[105] However, other local churches were alerted to this new tactic so that when a similar incident occurred at St Mary's Church, Bulwell, the authorities were prepared. As soon as the women started their chant of, "O God, save Annie Kenney, Sylvia Pankhurst and all women who are persecuted and suffer in prison for conscience sake. Amen," the service was suspended and men in the congregation set about ejecting the women who, although avoiding violence, made this as difficult as possible.

The background to these actions was the Archbishop of Canterbury's condemnation of hunger-striking and condoning force-feeding in 1913. This led to churches no longer being viewed as off-limits for direct action and the Nottingham WSPU also withdrew financial support from church causes.

---

[103] *Nottingham Daily Express,* 26.7.1913.
[104] Whitmore, R. (2007), p 179.
[105] *Nottingham Journal,* 17.11.1913.

Following this, there was nation-wide, renewed attack on post boxes, using corrosive liquid, resulting in a fire in a post box on Station Street. The *Nottingham Evening Post,* under the headline 'Hundreds of letters damaged, Pillar Box Outrages in Nottingham' reported:

> Another outrage of a dastardly character was perpetrated in Nottingham last evening by the militant suffragists, and on this occasion it again appears to have been carefully and elaborately planned. As on a previous occasion the women had sought to damage the letters in pillar boxes throughout the city by depositing tubes containing a black fluid which smelt like paint and methylated spirits. In additional to the tubes, which had some wadding and were enclosed in envelopes, a quantity of parchment paper covered with such ink as it would hold was also deposited in the boxes.
>
> The first intimation that an outrage had been committed was received shortly before seven o'clock, and information soon reached the head office that pillar boxes practically all over the town, and even at Basford and Bulwell, had been visited by the suffragists. Not satisfied with this, they had the audacity to direct their attention to the box at the General Post Office and altogether hundreds of letters were damaged.
>
> The glass tubes containing the fluid bore the inscriptions, 'Give us the vote, Mr Asquith', 'Lloyd George votes for women' and 'Bring in a government measure or get out', whilst in some cases, with the stock of tubes insufficient to go round, the fluid had been poured into foolscap envelopes, and deposited in the pillar boxes.
>
> The operations of the militants seemed to have taken place simultaneously between five and six o'clock, for the whole of the boxes were emptied about half past six.
>
> The officials at the Post Office immediately communicated with the police, who promptly instituted inquiries but, as will readily be understood, their task was an extremely difficult one.
>
> Fortunately, with few exceptions, the addresses were decipherable, and the letters were forwarded to their destinations the same evening. The boxes thus tampered with include those at the following places:-
>
> St Peter's-Gate
> The General Post Office in Queen Street
> The Rope Walk

Corner of Raleigh-street and Waverley-street
Corner of Broad-street and Parliament-street
Castle Street
Kirke White-street
Bulwell Post Office
Highbury-Vale, Bulwell[106]

Post boxes were again targeted on 22 December 1913, mostly outside the city centre, designed to cause maximum disruption during the pre-Christmas period. Some of the incendiary letters burst into flames when being sorted at the Queen Street General Post Office, but 'quick-thinking staff' used sand to extinguish them, so very little post was lost.[107]

The Grantham Journal, Saturday 27 June 1914, reported 'Further Pillar Box Outrages' in Nottingham:

> There were renewed outrages by suffragists in Nottingham on Tuesday night, when the greater portion of the letter boxes in the city were found to contain tubes of black fluid. Both in extent and consequences the raid was the most serious so far attempted locally, and, though most of the letters affected by the liquid will reach their destination, there were a few hopelessly damaged.

Final Actions

In the period from 1913 to the outbreak of war in August 1914, WSPU militancy became increasingly clandestine and violent, involving arson, bombs and physical attacks on members of the Government. In April 1913 a pavilion at a tennis club in the Park was set on fire and attributed to the suffragettes. Then there were two arson attacks in the county in 1914, one 19 February at Babbington Colliery and another on the Nottingham Corporation Dutch barn at Bulcote on 9 March, which caused £2,000 pounds worth of damage. Both were attributed to suffragette actions, but the evidence would

---
[106] *Nottingham Evening Post,* 7.2.1913.
[107] *Nottingham Evening Post,* 23.11.1913.

seem to be sketchy, at best. At Babbington, two hayricks were fired and 'evidence' found nearby consisting of suffragette periodicals (obtainable by anyone) and the curious slogan, 'It is fire that purifies', rather than the better-known and instantly identifiable suffragette slogans 'Votes for Women' and 'Deeds Not Words'. Similarly, the only evidence at the Bulcote barn fire consisted of Votes for Women leaflets.[108]

The escalation of militancy by the WSPU in Nottingham did not go unnoticed by the local NUWSS branch: Nellie Dowson, speaking at a garden party at Langley House, Mapperley Park, responded eloquently on the issue of militancy, as the following extract from the *Nottingham Evening Post* demonstrates:

> Referring to the militancy the speaker deprecated it entirely and spoke of the abhorrence with which she looked upon the crimes committed by the militant women, but she emphasized that they gave health and even life showing their intense belief in their cause. The idea that non-militant suffragists should cease endeavouring to obtain the vote by constitutional methods until the militant women had forsaken their violent tactics, she described as absurd.[109]

But potentially the most remarkable incident might have been the out-come of Eileen Casey's plans - although we will never know exactly what they were. Casey (1886 – after 1963), a WSPU member acting independently, was arrested on 24 June 1914, the day of the visit by King George V and Queen Mary to Nottingham, allegedly with bomb-making equipment in her bag:

> In her dress case… two bundles of fire-lighters, two pocket electric flash lamps, two boxes of matches, a small bottle of benzene, a glass cutter, a pair of pliers, a half inch chisel, a gardener's trowel, a road map of Derbyshire, a motor cycle road book of the British Isles, a street map of Nottingham with the Market-place marked out in pencil, a book of views of Derbyshire churches, including the one recently burned down in Breadsall, a book on Southwell Cathedral containing notes on the fly leaf showing the positions of the doors… three pocket knives, a box

---

[108] Two leaflets retrieved from the scene may be seen at Nottinghamshire Archives, ref: DD 2367/1/47/1-2.
[109] *Nottingham Evening Post*, 26.6.1914.

containing a quarter-pound packet of cheddite [an explosive], 90 feet of fuse, a box of fuse matches.[110]

The Nottingham newspapers had a field-day with the events surrounding her arrest and trial at Nottingham Guildhall on 26 June. She was held on remand until 8 July at Holloway Prison. After going on hunger strike she was forcibly-fed by nasal tube at least 46 times at Holloway and subsequently at Winson Green Prison in Birmingham. Casey was sentenced to fifteen months' imprisonment on 28 July, but was released soon after under the general amnesty afforded to suffragette prisoners at the outbreak of the War. Eileen Casey is an example of a woman working alone and outside the main framework of the WSPU as the suffrage campaign was coming to an end. It is highly unlikely that the local WSPU branch was aware of her intentions.[111]

War

In 1914, Liberal preparations began for the General Election and, for the first time, women's suffrage was to be addressed. David Lloyd George and other sympathetic ministers opened discussions with leading members of the NUWSS, proposing the introduction of a new Reform Bill. These negotiations were interrupted by the outbreak of war in August. The war threatened to split the NUWSS as many of the suffragists on its National Executive were pacifists and internationalists, whilst their leader, Millicent Fawcett, was an ardent nationalist and patriot. In line with the WSPU, whose leaders Emmeline and Christabel Pankhurst embraced the war and patriotism, the NUWSS also suspended campaigning, albeit temporarily, and members diverted their energies to the organisation of various relief programmes. In August 1914 an independent local body, the Women's Defence Relief Corps, was established

---

[110] *Nottingham Evening Post*, 2.7.2014, Special Edition.
[111] See *Women of Australia*, National Centre of Biography, Australia National University, for a comprehensive overview of Casey's life.

in Nottingham, made up from five different women's suffrage societies. Their purpose was to give assistance to families and to keep a register of suitable women willing to volunteer and train for Special Constable duties, in case of emergency. The Corps also offered first aid and signaling classes for members and worked with the British Red Cross.[112]

The Vote, at last!

In 1918 the Representation of the People Act was passed, enabling women over the age of thirty to vote for the first time - women who were householders or wives of householders, occupiers of property of £5 annual value, or graduates of a British university, including those who had fulfilled the qualifications but were not allowed to graduate.

Alice Dowson wrote triumphantly in her diary: "The Women's Suffrage has become an accomplished fact! The result of so many years labour."[113]

Her granddaughter, Dame Alex Meynell, added: "It tends… to be assumed that it was what women did in the war that got them the vote, and not the long campaign of the Suffra*gists* starting in the 1860s, or the actions of the Suffra*gettes* in the 1900s. The Suffragists of Nottingham were in no doubt about the importance of their contribution…"[114]

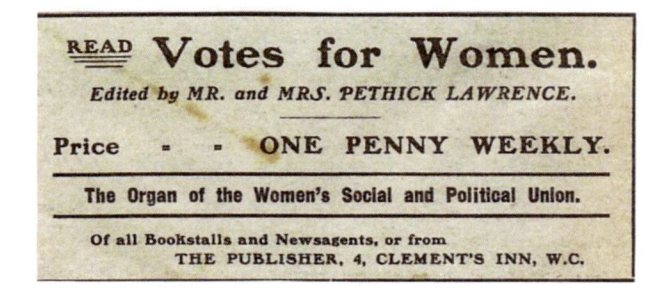

READ Votes for Women.
Edited by MR. and MRS. PETHICK LAWRENCE.

Price   -   -   ONE PENNY WEEKLY.

The Organ of the Women's Social and Political Union.

Of all Bookstalls and Newsagents, or from
THE PUBLISHER, 4, CLEMENT'S INN, W.C.

---

[112] Nottinghamshire Archives, ref: DD PP 4/1, 4/2-8.
[113] Meynell (1998), p 258.
[114] *ibid*

Local Stories

May BURGIS (1874-1930)

Born Catharine Mary 'May' Burgis at Blewbury, Berkshire in 1874, May was the eldest child of John James Burgis and his wife Hannah Maria Stevens. In 1891 the family living in Besington, Oxfordshire, where John Burgis was a grocer. May was then sixteen and a scholar/ teacher. Her siblings were Edith, Helen, Frank Thomas, William Gainford, John, Kate, Frederick and Nora Gainford. Another child, George, was born later that year.

John Burgis died in 1894 but seems to have left his family provided for as his widow Hannah was 'living on own means' on the 1901 Census, when the family were at 32 Upper Redlands Rd, Reading in Berkshire. May was twenty-six when her father died and a 'teacher on own account' (i.e. in private rather than Council schools) and her sister Kate was also a teacher. It seems likely that May, at least, moved to Nottingham in 1901 where she would work for the Nottingham Education Committee for twenty-nine years.

She became an active suffragette at around the same time as Helen Watts (see below) and was elected as Honorary Secretary of the WSPU branch in Nottingham in 1908, an office she held until 1912. On 24 February 1909, May was present when Helen was arrested outside the House of Commons in London. In a letter to Helen[115] she describes herself as feeling "a desperate coward" because she had escaped the worst of the conflict whilst Helen had "suffered so terribly for the Cause."

May evaded the Census in 1911, but her mother Hannah, sister Kate and brother George were at home at 21 Chaucer Street. May taught at Mundella Grammar School for some years before becoming Headmistress of Clarendon School for Girls in 1925, where she was greatly respected.

---

[115] Nottinghamshire Archives DD 893/3/29

On 26 April 1930 Catharine May Burgis BA died at home after a short illness at 4 Whittingham Road, Mapperley. *Nottingham Evening Post* (28 April) stated that she was a most efficient headmistress, held in the highest esteem by her colleagues and all the pupils. The funeral was held at St Jude's Church, Mapperley, on 30 April and it merited a long article in the *Evening Post* later that day.

Rev E. A. Dunn conducted the service which was attended by aldermen, councillors, representatives of the Education Committee and several teachers' organisations. In attendance was also a Miss Moncriff of University College London (where we assume May studied for her degree) plus staff and seventy pupils from Clarendon School. Mr Syson the head and Miss Holehouse, a teacher, of Huntingdon Street School were also there. May's family included Rev & Mrs W. G. Burgis, Miss Helen Burgis, Mrs Freeman (Kate), Miss Nora Burgis and Frederick Burgis. Her body was taken to Leicester for cremation. At no point was there any mention of May's early WSPU involvement.

In the *Nottingham Evening Post* on 16 December 1931, it was noted that a little 17th century carved figure in boxwood had been presented to the Manning School in memory of the late Catharine Burgis by her sisters. Clarendon School had become the Manning School for Girls that year.

Alice DAX (1878-1959)

Alice Mary Mills was born in Liverpool in 1878, one of seven children of a Harbour Board clerk. The family struggled financially and according to her friend Enid Hilton, her mother's hard life caused Alice to have a "formidable hatred for [her] father and men in general." Alice worked in the post office in Liverpool and was reputedly an active suffragette. She married fellow-Liverpudlian Henry Richard Dax at Toxteth Park in 1905. He already had a business as a chemist and oculist in Eastwood, Nottinghamshire, and Alice joined him there. They became friends with William and Sallie Hopkin, forward thinking socialists who gathered like-minded people around them in Eastwood, including the young D. H. Lawrence and several of his friends.

Enid Hilton, the Hopkins' daughter, recalled:

> "She and my mother worked for the women's cause and I remember being taken to meetings in the City of Nottingham. We waved green, purple and white flags and the speakers, the Pankhursts, Annie Kenny and others whose names I have forgotten – came home with us and stayed at our house, and discussions went on far into the night, intense, but friendly... Alice Dax carried her ideas almost to extremes. Gradually she became a NAME in the district, a person to whom people turned in trouble, and who initiated all the good community enterprises, such as nursing associations, local forms of health insurance and so forth. Alice

Dax was one of the kindest persons I have ever met, but most of the men of her generation feared her." [116]

Alice's forthright manner and her "loud laugh" did not endear her to the narrow society of Eastwood. "She and Sally Hopkin both refused to festoon their windows with traditional Nottingham lace curtains, and local people threatened to stone the windows."[117] Alice didn't care what people thought and was also unafraid to stand up and speak her mind at meetings – the following advertisement appeared in the *Derby Daily Telegraph* on Saturday 12 January 1907:

> At 6.30 Sunday in Socialists' Hall (up Wildsmith's Passage), Full-street, address by Mrs Alice Dax of Eastwood on 'The inequality of the sexes and its reason.' Questions allowed.

Trade dropped off at the chemist's shop due to Alice's political activities and the shop was bought by Boots in the summer of 1910. They moved their business to 29 Station Street, Shirebrook (Dax's Corner) where their friends continued to visit them. D H Lawrence was one of them, and he was to come to know Alice very well; in 1910 she visited him in London and in 1911 he stayed with the family in Shirebrook. Lawrence frequently put people he knew into his books, and strong aspects of Alice's character are to be found in the suffragette Clara Dawes in his first novel, *Sons and Lovers*, which was published the following year, and Kate Leslie in *The Plumed Serpent*.

From the 1940s Alice and Henry lived at Little Oaks, Lindhurst Lane, Mansfield. In their seventies, they emigrated to Australia where their son Eric, an eminent psychiatrist, already lived. Alice died in Preston, Australia, in 1959.

---

[116] *The Priest of Love* by Harry T. Moore, quoted in: Dix, C. (1980), *D. H. Lawrence and Women*.
[117] Referred to in Hilton, E. (1993), *More Than One Life, A Nottinghamshire Childhood with D. H. Lawrence*, p 22.

Helena 'Nellie' DOWSON (1866-1964)

Helena Brownsword was born in October 1866, the only daughter of Alderman Anderson and Jeanie Brownsword, both influential people in Nottingham. Her father served on the Council from 1886 and was Sheriff in 1890-91, then Mayor in 1892-93. He was a silk merchant and Chairman of three companies including the City Tramways, while Jeannie Brownsword was the first woman member of the Nottingham Board of Guardians 1895-1907. Helena also had an elder brother, Anderson H. Brownsword, and the family lived in Chestnut House on Mapperley Road.

In July 1894 Helena married William Enfield Dowson (Will), the eldest son of Benjamin and Alice Dowson. Alice was actively concerned with social and political issues and Helena, or 'Nellie' as she was affectionately known, seems to have been very close to her mother-in-law and sisters-in-law Maud, Hilda and Lina, working unstintingly with them for the cause of women's suffrage. In 1894 Alice Dowson had become Secretary of the Nottingham Branch of Women's Suffrage but when her health deteriorated Nellie took over the work around August 1896, because, as Alice observed: "[She] was ready, willing, enthusiastic and young" (Meynell, 1998). That same year, Alice's diaries tell us that Nellie accompanied her sister-in-law Maud to a suffrage meeting in Birmingham; whilst in 1900 she succeeded in persuading her mother-in-law to take the chair at Nottingham Women's Suffrage annual meeting (Meynell, 1998).

Along with members of her extended family (all the men and women of the Dowson family were politically engaged and supportive of women's suffrage) Nellie continued to attend suffrage meetings, including two large meetings in Nottingham in 1907, one of which was addressed by Christabel Pankhurst. Then in June 1908, she travelled to a suffrage event in London with a party of thirty or more from Nottingham, including three of her sisters-in-law and a brother-in-law. The event involved marches and speeches and was attended by 10,000 people, mostly women of all ages and from all classes and was deemed a great success, although, disappointingly, it prompted no action from the Government.

The following year, on 5 July 1909, the National Union of Women's Suffrage Societies organised a mass meeting in Nottingham Market-place. Although the police had been informed of the event and had promised to attend, they failed to turn up and the meeting was unruly and even violent with anti-suffrage feeling running high. As Honorary Secretary of the Nottingham Branch, Nellie sent a letter of protest to the local paper about the behaviour of the police. Two of the speakers, Eleanor Rathbone and Edward Carpenter, who had been unable to speak because of the hostility and disruptive actions of a section of the crowd, stayed with Nellie and Will at their house, 'Felixstowe', in The Park, which had been passed on to them by Will's parents in 1906 when they retired to a more rural setting in Upper Broughton.

Nellie continued to be an active suffragist. For example, in 1909 alone she hosted an 'at home' event where she gave a well-received speech, organised a fund-raising lunch, attended numerous meetings - one at Caxton Hall in London - and worked in the Suffrage Shop in Nottingham. 1910 was General Election year – in fact there were two, because the January election resulted in a 'hung' Parliament, so a second was held in December. Nellie and her sisters-in-law again worked tirelessly, promoting the cause of women's suffrage by organising meetings in towns and villages around Nottingham. On Polling Days in January (elections were not single-day affairs before the First World War) they attended the polling booths to gather signatures for petitions and faced hostility and abuse as well as inclement weather. Again, there was disappointment from the point of view of women's suffrage but, undaunted, activity continued, although the pace of campaigning naturally reduced after the election.

The Women's Suffrage Shop on Long Row continued to operate, and a meeting was arranged for March in the Mechanics Hall, Nottingham. On 9 July, Nellie was one of the organisers of a large group travelling to London to support the 2nd reading of the Conciliation Bill, so-called because part of its aim was to unite suffrage supporters from all parties. In addition to all this, that summer Felixstowe was one of the venues for a day-long garden party which featured, among other events, a play about women's suffrage.

Not surprisingly, Nellie was also present at the 40,000-strong Coronation Procession on 17 June 1911 (see flyer on cover); whilst in January 1913 she attended the Houses of Parliament with her husband Will and his sister Maud to hear the reading of the 'Grey Amendment', only to hear Asquith withdraw the whole suffrage bill, causing despair and disappointment. Later that year, Nellie and Maud took part in the Suffrage Pilgrimage to London, joining it as it passed through Nottinghamshire.

After the long campaign for women's suffrage had finally proved successful, the suffragists of Nottingham acknowledged Nellie's tireless contribution to the cause in an illuminated address (below), presented to her under her formal name Helena B. Dowson. It reads:

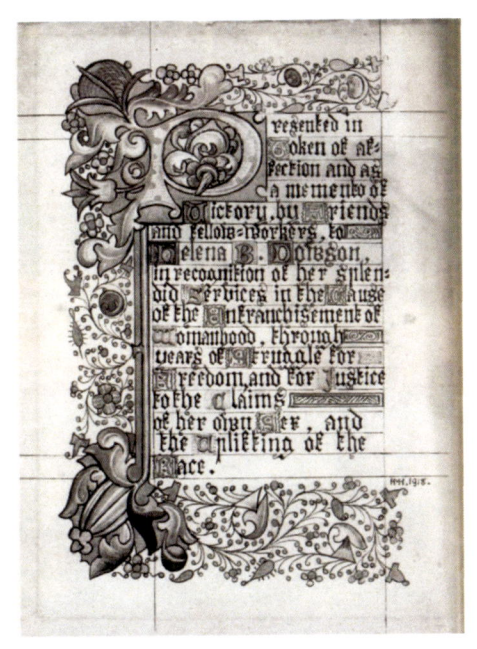

"[I]n token of affection and as a memento of Victory by Friends and Fellow-Workers, in recognition of her splendid Services in the Cause of the Enfranchisement of Womanhood, through years of Struggle for Freedom and for Justice for the Claims of her own Sex and the Uplifting of the Race."[118]

However, Nellie did not rest on her laurels; in 1920 she was the first woman to become a Justice of the Peace in Nottingham after the Sex Disqualification Removal Act was passed, and the same year she became the first Liberal woman to gain a seat on Nottingham City Council, representing the Meadows Ward. She went on to become a President of the East Nottingham Women's Liberal Association as well as Vice President of the Nottingham Liberal Union. She died at the age of ninety-eight in October 1964 at Northfield, Newby Bridge, Ulverston, Lancashire.[119]

---

[118] Meynell, A. *Public Servant, Private Woman*, photograph opp. p 97.
[119] Obituary of Helena Dowson, *Nottinghamshire Guardian* 3.10.1964.

Elsie HOWEY (1884-1963)

Rose Elsie Howey was born 1 December 1884 at the Rectory, Finningley, which was then in Nottinghamshire. She was the younger daughter of Thomas Howey, Rector of Holy Trinity Church and his wife Gertrude Oldfield. Elsie's elder sister Mary was born in 1882. Thomas died in a riding accident in March 1887 and is buried in the churchyard. Gertrude moved with her two young daughters to Cradley, near Malvern in Worcestershire, where they were to live for the rest of their lives.

At some point all three women espoused the suffrage cause, though it was Elsie who became the militant one. In 1902 she enrolled at St Andrews University but left in 1904 for Germany where she became aware of women's political disadvantages. When she returned to Britain she became an active member of the WSPU, travelling around the country speaking on platforms and agitating at political meetings.

She was first arrested along with her sister Mary in February 1908 and imprisoned for six weeks but as soon as she was released Elsie was agitating again and was arrested outside the Houses of Parliament on 30 June, sentenced this time to three months. When she was released on 16 September she was escorted in a carriage drawn by fifty women in suffragette colours to Queen's Hall and presented with an illuminated scroll of honour.

For a time, Elsie worked in the West Country as a paid WSPU organiser in Torquay and Paignton. However, she was still travelling up to London to take part in the big events and demonstrations and on 16 April 1909 she appeared for the first time dressed as Joan of Arc, in full armour, mounted on a white horse at the head of the procession which escorted Mrs Pethick Lawrence on her release from prison. The suffragists would often march with banners depicting famous women like St Hilda, Florence Nightingale, Boudicca and Queen Elizabeth I, the elaborate costumes and floats designed by the Artist's Suffrage League, and Joan of Arc[120] became a potent symbol of courage and self-sacrifice in the suffrage campaign and made regular appearances – not always played by the same person.

After her arrest on 20 July 1909, Elsie fasted for 144 hours and was one of the first suffragettes to be force-fed. This became a habitual means of protest for her. The following January, although hardly recovered from her ordeal, she was arrested again and sentenced to six weeks hard labour and for this she received the Holloway medal from Mrs Pankhurst (a silver portcullis + arrow). Not surprisingly, her health suffered severely. Her mother wrote in 1928 that Elsie had been rendered almost dumb from injuries inflicted on her throat by forced feeding and that: "her beautiful voice was ruined." Other suffragettes would also suffer permanent damage to their health.

We don't hear much about Mary Howey until the 1911 Census: as already mentioned many suffragettes went missing on Census night or refused to fill in the form as a protest. Elsie and her mother Gertrude were evaders but Mary, at home at Holly Lodge, Cradley, was a resister; declaring herself to be an artist and suffragette, she also wrote VOTES FOR WOMEN in large, elegant letters across the Census form.

In March 1912, Elsie broke two windows at Liberty's shop in Regent Street and was back in jail for four months; then again in December that year, when she became so ill that questions were asked in Parliament and a friend insisted on paying her fine and had her released – but not before her teeth had been broken by a sadistic doctor during forced feeding.

In June 1913, she bravely played the role of Joan of Arc once more, accompanying the coffin of her friend, Emily Wilding Davidson, who died under the hooves of the King's horse at the Derby; but after that she disappeared from public life. She died fifty years later, on 13 March 1963, giving instructions that there was to be no funeral service and no memorial. Her sister Mary died in 1967.

---

[120] Joan of Arc was in the news because she was beatified by the Pope that year; she would become a saint in 1920.

Edith Annie LEES (1881-1964)

Edith was born in March 1881 and was one month old when the 1881Census was taken. She was the eldest daughter of Charles Joseph Mee and Annie Ellen Baker, then living at 37 Derby Road, though the family home would later become a substantial property on Daybook Vale.

She married John Martin Lees on 11 September 1902 at St Paul's Church, Daybrook. John was the eldest son of John Lees of Ivy Mount, Mansfield Road and the family business was Lees, the haberdashers and small-wear manufacturers in Carlton Street. Edith and John had three children: John (1903), Mavis (1905) and Wendy (1912).

The couple's fathers were both involved in local politics as councilors and aldermen, and at some point Edith became involved in women's suffrage. In her scrapbook is a newspaper article from 6 February 1911 about a Resolution that had been passed in favour of Women's Suffrage by Nottingham Council. Another significant article, dated 5 May 1911, concerns the 'Pageant of Great Women' written by Cicely Hamilton, which came on tour to the Mechanics Institute for two performances on 4 May, facilitated by the local WSPU branch. As well as the London cast which included well-known members of the Actresses Franchise League, seventy Nottingham women took part. A photograph in Edith's album shows a scene from the production with a small boy marked with an X who is probably John Lees Jnr. It was also reported that during the evening, "a ladies string orchestra under the conductorship of Miss E. Burgis played several selections."[121]

---

[121] Unattributed newspaper cutting in scrapbook

Edith does not appear on the Census for 1911, so she may have been an evader. The following year, on 4 March 1912, she was arrested for 'wilful damage' after breaking windows in London. This was a massive, well-co-ordinated campaign: perfectly respectable woman arrived at their designated place, took hammers from their muffs and reticules and – to the best of their ability – smashed the windows of various department stores, banks and other public buildings. This was deliberate act of provocation – most simply waited to be arrested and the police were ready to oblige. Edith gave a false name – 'Annie Baker' (her mother's maiden name) - to save any embarrassment or adverse publicity at home. She wrote to her husband from prison, "A lady and I broke four windows in Weldon's – about 6ft by 2ft – and we were pounced on at once. It isn't 8 o'clock yet. We thought we would get it over before the roughs came." So she and her companion were amongst the first to act and be arrested.

She was bound over for £5 to appear at Bow Street Magistrates Court on 5 March, and then for trial at Kensington on 19 March on the sureties of Thomas Lamartine Yates (a solicitor married to a suffragette) and Mary Henrietta Graham for the large sum of £200. She appears to have been discharged on 26th. She was pregnant with her youngest daughter at the time, which probably explains her early release. Only a fraction of the prisoners were named in the newspapers – there were at least 150 arrests - and 'Annie Baker' has not been found among them; but she appears on the Roll of Honour of Suffragette Prisoners 1905-1914.

Edith became a founder member of the Nottingham branch of the National Council of Women, as did many ex-suffragists and suffragettes, to further the cause of women. At a meeting of the Nottingham Efficiency Club on 8 Dec 1920, speaking on the subject 'Women in Business', she said, "Women are out to stay in the business world, and in my opinion, it is to the benefit of the world in general that they should. When they have more lady members of Parliament they will be able to use their influence in the right way."[122]

Edith Lees died on 30 January 1964, aged 82. She is buried at Wilford Hill Cemetery, Nottingham.

---

[122] Unattributed newspaper cutting in scrapbook.

Sarah Barker MERRICK (1869-1933)

Born Sarah Babbs in 1869 at Whittington Moor, Derby, she first came to Hucknall as a young teacher at Beardall Street Infant School in 1887. After two years of college training she became head teacher at Morton Infant School near Tibshelf. In 1894 Sarah married Joseph William Merrick, also a teacher, and they lived at Walsall and Upper Broughton, where they may have known the Dowsons, before returning to Hucknall in 1899 when Joseph became headmaster of Butler's Hill School. They lived at The Knoll on Beardall Street.

In 1910 Nellie Dowson held a suffrage meeting in Hucknall and by 1913 Sarah was running the local branch of the NUWSS over a teashop on High Street. Her obituary states that she "played a very active part in public life. Her keen sympathy with the cause of women led her to associate herself with the suffragette (*sic*) movement and on several occasions she joined in the demonstrations in London, when the cause was far from popular."

It continues:

> Knowledge and insight which she acquired by secretarial work for the British Women's Temperance Society ultimately led her to become a candidate for a seat on the Basford Board of Guardians in the Labour Party's interest. Mrs Merrick thus became the first lady member of that now defunct body, and she put up a stern fight for better conditions for the poor and needy. In the same party's interest she fought for a seat on the County Council, but was defeated in the West Ward by the late Mr William Moss who had held the seat for many years. Since then two or three women have succeeded entering that august assembly.
>
> In wider political work she assisted Messrs Carter, Varley and Spencer in their election campaigns by speech and work and occasionally addressed election meetings in Nottingham. Perhaps the most intriguing feature of her activity lay in the fact that her husband was a leading official of the Liberal Party – no doubt with Radical leanings and much sympathy with the best elements of the Labour Party.

Mrs Merrick was also for many years associated with the Adult School movement, being at one time President of the Women's Branch at Hucknall, and at the time of her death Minutes Secretary for the County. The League of Nations Union also found her a sincere worker for all its efforts... Mrs Merrick's independence of mind and thought showed itself also in her religious views.[123]

Sarah Merrick died in Mount Vernon Lodge nursing home, Waverley Street, Nottingham on 16 Oct 1933, aged 65. Her funeral service was conducted at home and at the graveside by a neighbour, Rev W. F. Scott, and she is buried in Hucknall Cemetery, grave no.1598.

Lady Laura RIDDING (1849-1939)

Suffragists came from all classes of society but one wonders if many members of the Church of England in Nottinghamshire realised the depth of political commitment held by their Bishop's wife. Lady Laura Palmer was born into the aristocracy in 1849 – her father was the 1st Earl of Shelbourne. When she was twenty-seven she married Rev George Ridding, a widower twenty years her senior who was then headmaster of Winchester College. She was already an advocate of women's suffrage and involved in rescue work with women, nursing and the temperance movement.

In 1884, George Ridding became the first Bishop of Southwell and they moved to Nottingham. How political was the wife of a Bishop allowed to be in the 1880s? With her husband's support, Laura was able to put her energy and expertise into many campaigns for the benefit of women locally. They founded a rescue home for girls caught in prostitution, campaigned for better conditions for women factory

---

[123] *Hucknall Dispatch*, 19.10.1933

workers and Laura was very much involved with the Girls' Evening Home Movement – clubs for young women to keep them off the streets and out of the pubs after work.[124] She was also responsible for founding Family Care, a busy organisation still supporting Nottingham families today. She was a Poor Law Guardian and rural district councillor for the Southwell Union from 1895-1904, and one of the founders of the National Union of Women Workers in 1895, the first trade union for women. During WW1 she was active in the Soldiers' & Sailors' Family Association, the Women's War Agricultural Committee and the YWCA.

When Bishop Ridding died in 1904, Lady Laura was free to pursue whatever cause she chose and her name appears as one of the patrons of a Fete held in aid of the East Midland Federation of the National Union of Woman's Suffrage Societies in 1912, though she had moved back to Hampshire, by then. She was a great organiser, philanthropist and author who wrote regularly for *The Times* on subjects like women's education.

She died in 1939 and was brought back to Southwell to be buried with her husband. They lie beside the south door outside the Minster.

---

[124] See: Edlin-White, R. *Spinster of No Occupation? Mary Ellen Shaw: 1859-1926*

Muriel Carey WALLIS (1882–1929)

Muriel was born on 25 February 1882, the eldest daughter of George Harry Wallis FSA and Katherine 'Kate' Watson Carey. They lived at The Residence, Nottingham Castle, where her father was Director of the Art Gallery for fifty years. The Carey family was very much involved in social issues in Nottingham, including women's suffrage. Kate Wallis appears on the list of Patrons for the East Midland Federation Fete in 1912, alongside her sister, Henrietta Carey.

Muriel was active in the WSPU from about 1907 and took part in several London processions, 1909-1911. She was arrested for 'wilfully obstructing Police whilst in the execution of their duty' on Black Friday, 18 Nov 1910, at the Deputation to Parliament. Bailed for £2, she was bound over to keep the peace but not imprisoned. Christabel Pankhurst wrote personally to thank her for taking part and hoped "the ill usage to which you were subjected has not seriously harmed you." She was almost certainly an evader on the 1911 Census.

In her scrapbook is a newspaper article about a meeting held at Morley's Café on 22 March 1911, at which the speaker, Mrs Simon Massey, said the Census offered "an excellent and most logical method of protest." Mr C. L. Rothera was there to advise that a penalty of £5 could be imposed for resisting or evading; and if payment was refused the defendant's goods might be impounded – or if they had none, seven days imprisonment was likely. Many women thought it was well worth the risk.[125] According to Michael Austin, Muriel was also involved with the Church League for Women's Suffrage, a branch of which was established in Nottingham in 1913 (Austin 2014, p 141).

Muriel died on 21 January 1929 at 26 The Ropewalk. Her obituary in the *Nottingham Evening Post* (23 January) noted that "Miss Wallis was well known in the district, and engaged herself in social and philanthropic work on

---

[125] Our thanks to Margaret Rizk for this information extracted from Muriel's suffrage scrapbook which was then in a private collection.

an extensive scale." She certainly was - she was a member of the National Council of Women and a member of the General Council of the YWCA, having been connected with this latter organisation for over 25 years. She was also a member of the Guild of Helpers, closely associated with the work of the Nottingham and Notts. Convalescent Homes and the Social Guild.

In 1914 when girls employed in the lace trade were thrown out of work, she opened a shop on Derby Road for social work which was so successful that a number of girls were quickly found employment manufacturing unbreakable dolls, for which a small factory was run in Park-passage (now the Eastern end of Lenton Road, next to the Castle) until 1922.

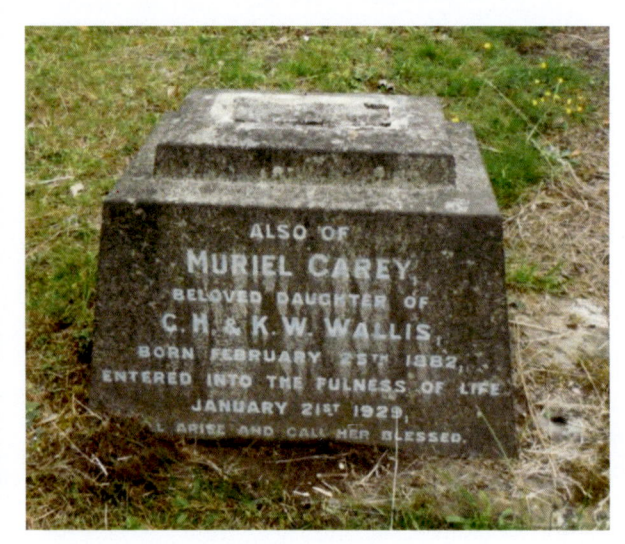

As was the case with several of her friends, no mention was made in her obituary of her suffrage work.

Her funeral service took place on 24 January at St James' Church, Standard Hill (now demolished), conducted by Canon Gem. Amongst the mourners was her friend, May Burgis.

She is buried in the Carey plot at the Church (Rock) Cemetery.

Helen Kirkpatrick WATTS (1881-1972)

Helen Watts is one of Nottingham's best-known suffragettes. She was born on 13 July 1881 at Bishopswearmouth, Co. Durham, the eldest child of Rev Alan Hunter Watts and his wife Ethelinda Woodrow Cassels. He became vicar of Holy Trinity Lenton in 1893. There were seven younger siblings including Alice Margaret (1882), Nevile Hunter (1883) and Ethelinda Bertha (1886). Helen seems to have been particularly close to her brother Nevile. They published a volume of poetry together in 1906 entitled *Poems by a Brother and Sister*.

Helen joined the WSPU after hearing Christabel Pankhurst speak at Circus Street Hall on 9 December 1907. This was a follow-up to the volatile meeting a week earlier at the Mechanics Institute, when pandemonium broke out and Miss Pankhurst and her colleagues struggled for an hour to make themselves heard (see pp 16-17). At this second, women-only, meeting, Helen heard the message loud and clear and was determined to become fully involved.

Her family only realised the full depth of her commitment when she was arrested outside the House of Commons on 24 February 1909 for causing 'wilful obstruction'. She wrote to them that evening to warn them that her arrest would undoubtedly be in the newspapers next day.

Her mother replied:

> "I cannot say that your letter was altogether a surprise to me! For it had crossed my mind once or twice before that you might think it was your duty to do as you have done - But I am only very sorry that you should have suffered so much quietly for so long - ! I wish you had told me about it long ago. Of course Father and I are proud of you..."[126]

In court, she was bound over to keep the peace but she refused and was sentenced to one month in Holloway Gaol. When news of her imprisonment was known, messages of support flooded in and on her release she received an enthusiastic reception at Morley's Café on Wheeler Gate on 24 March 1909.

She was arrested again on 4 September 1909 in Leicester with Mary Rawson, another woman from Nottingham, at a meeting addressed by Winston Churchill. The charge was 'disorderly conduct' -simply for trying to enter the building. In Leicester Gaol Helen went on hunger strike for ninety hours. She was threatened with force-feeding but it didn't happen and she was released after five days. She received a medal from the WSPU for her hunger strike but she protested that she had done very little compared with some of the others.

At the celebratory welcome home meeting on the 17 of September at Morley's Café she made her first public speech:

> "Prison is a school in which we learn to understand what friendship and comradeship mean... above all what liberty means. We come to see that liberty is the greatest thing in the world and the passion for liberty is the strongest inspiration to action and effort that the world has known. We must come down from the various little pedestals on which we have been mounted by birth and education and forget everything but the fact that we are... fighting for a human right."

By 1912 Helen was training to be a nurse at the Royal National Hospital in Bath. Later, she joined the Civil Service - her death certificate records, "Clerk (Ministry of Pensions) retired." Meanwhile, on the 1911 Census, her sister Alice was listed as 'Secretary of Suffragist Society'. The Watts family left Nottingham for Brighton in 1917 when Alan Watts took up a new post.

---

[126] The quotations in this section are extracted from copies of Helen Watts' papers which are held in Nottinghamshire Archives, ref: DD 893. Location of the originals is unknown.

After her retirement, Helen lived at Hassocks in Sussex. In May 1962, she gave an interview in Bath. She had come to see the remains of the 'Suffragette's Wood' at Eagle House, Batheaston, where she had stayed in 1911. Owned by the Blathwayte family, it was a place of convalescence for suffragettes who had been in prison. Whilst there, they all planted commemorative trees and Helen planted a juniper on 17 March 1911.[127] She told the reporter that she had carried a sprig of juniper from her tree ever since and that she was looking forward to a meeting with other members of the Suffragettes Fellowship (see p 73) in London on 14 July, the anniversary of Emmeline Pankhurst's birthday.[128]

In October 1965, aged 84, Helen emigrated to Canada[129] to join her sister Ethel, a teacher, and brother Frank; but ill-health forced her to return. She died in Wells, Somerset, on 18 August 1972 and is buried in St Vigor's churchyard at Stratton-on-the-Fosse.

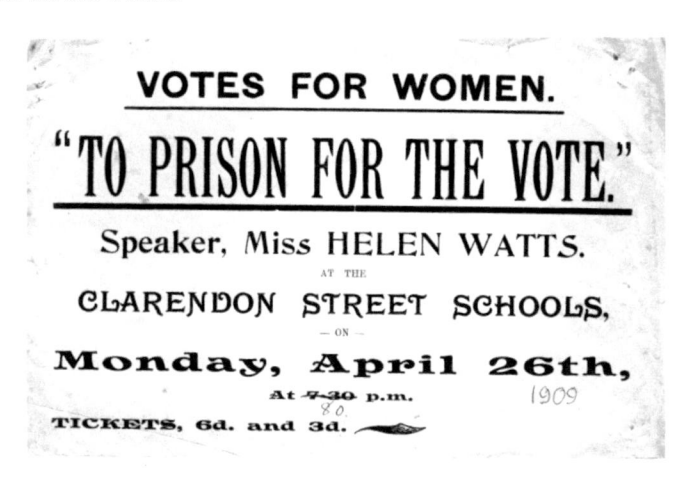

VOTES FOR WOMEN.
"TO PRISON FOR THE VOTE."
Speaker, Miss HELEN WATTS.
AT THE
CLARENDON STREET SCHOOLS,
ON
Monday, April 26th,
At 7-30 p.m. 1909
TICKETS, 6d. and 3d.

---

[127] The Howey sisters also planted trees: Elsie's was a Caucasian fir (2 May 1910) and Mary's a Cypress (2 Sept. 1910). For the complete list see Dobbie, B. M. W. (1979) *A Nest of Suffragettes in Somerset.* Batheaston Society.
[128] *Bath & Wells Evening Chronicle,* 18.5.1963.
[129] The photograph on p 69, taken at the time of her emigration, and the flyer on this page are from Helen's scrapbook and used courtesy of the Watts family.

Alice ZIMMERN (1855-1939)

Born in Postern Street on 22 September 1855, Alice Louisa Theodora Zimmern was the youngest of three clever sisters, the children of a German Jewish lace merchant, Hermann Theodore Zimmern and his wife Antonia Marie Therese Regina Leo. The Zimmerns had settled in Nottingham in 1850 with their eldest daughter Helen, who had been born in Hamburg in 1846. Another daughter, Antonia, was born in 1854.

It is difficult to say how long the Zimmerns stayed in Nottingham, but Alice was educated at Bedford College in London before going to Girton College, Cambridge, to study classics, a subject she taught in a number of schools, including Tunbridge Wells High School 1888-1891. In 1893 she won a Gilchrist Travelling Scholarship to America where she studied methods of education, particularly for women and girls. In 1898 she published *The Renaissance of Girls' Education in England: a Record of Fifty Years' Progress.*

Alice was a pacifist and a suffragist. She was always interested in women's rights and, though not militant herself, she recognised the fact that such tactics could be effective. Her main contribution was a book called *Women's Suffrage in Many Lands* (1909), an overview of the suffrage campaign across the world, which coincided with the Fourth Congress of the International Women's Suffrage (available to read on-line).

In later life in London, she dedicated herself to social and educational work, dying in Hampstead on 22 March 1939. There is a blue plaque on her former home in Lissenden Gardens, NW5, which commemorates her as a "pioneering advocate for women's education and suffrage." Girton College holds some of her personal papers and she is remembered by the Alice Zimmern Memorial Prize for Classics.

The Suffragette Fellowship

When the first – albeit partial – vote was won in 1918, the suffragettes did not disband. They continued to meet as the Suffragette Fellowship and continued to campaign for the full vote, which would take another ten years. As they all grew older, the remnant kept the faith, pursuing women's rights through their newspaper, *Calling All Women,* and lobbying Parliament on women's issues. In 1965 they began planning a 'Memorial to the Rank and File Suffrage Workers'. The bronze sculpture, by Edwin Russell, was finally unveiled in 1970 in Christchurch Gardens, Victoria, London.

The inscription reads:

"This tribute is erected by the Suffragette Fellowship to commemorate the courage and perseverance of all those men and women who in the long struggle for votes for women selflessly braved derision, opposition and ostracism, many enduring physical violence and suffering."

The Suffragette Fellowship disbanded in 1972. Their archive may be found in the Museum of the City of London.

Photo by Rob Edlin-White, 2017

Nottinghamshire Roll of Honour

The following names are of those women known to have been active in the Edwardian suffrage movement in Nottingham and its environs – can you add any others? If so, please let us know!

NUWSS & Church League for Women's Suffrage

Louisa M. Barringer, Mansfield
Mrs W. H. Blandy, Southwell
Alice Dowson
Maud Dowson
Helena 'Nellie' Dowson *nee* Brownsword
Hilda Dowson
Hannah Guilford
Mary Hoskyns, Southwell
Emily Manners *nee* Barringer, Mansfield
Sarah Merrick, Hucknall
Leonora Shaw
Valentia Smith, Southwell
Ethel Wainwright, Mansfield
Mrs Wallis, Mansfield
Alice Watts
Ethel Watts
Miss Willton, Mansfield
Louisa Wright, Mansfield

WSPU

Catherine Mary 'May' Burgis
Mrs Goodliffe
Miss Greenhall
Elsie Hall
Lillian Hicking

Mrs F. E. Hill *nee* Mayer[130]
Elsie Howey
Mary Howey
Miss S. Hutchinson
Edith Annie Lees
Julie Mayer
Elsa Oswald
Dorothy Pethick
Mary Rawson
Gladys Roberts[131]
Mrs Mary Thorpe
Muriel Carey Wallis
Helen Kirkpatrick Watts

Paid WSPU organisers in Nottingham

Rachel Barrett 1908
Nellie Crocker 1909-1912
Charlotte Marsh 1913

---

[130] Mrs Hill was chair of the Nottingham Standing Conference of Women's Organisations.
[131] A former Solicitor's Clerk who resided at 6 Carlton St, she was imprisoned in 1909 & 1911 for breaking Post Office windows. Referred to in relationship to the Suffragette Handkerchief which was embroidered by suffragettes in prison and can be viewed on www.sussexpast.co.uk

Bibliography

Austin, M. (2014) *Like a Swift Hurricane: People, Clergy and Class in a Midlands Diocese 1914-1919*. Chesterfield: Merton Priory Press.

Bounds, J. (2014) *A Song of Their Own: The fight for votes for women in Ipswich*. Stroud: The History Press.

Clements S. (2008) *Feminism, Citizenship and Social Activity: The role and importance of Local Women's Organisations, Nottingham 1918-1969*, Unpublished Dissertation, University of Nottingham.

Crawford E. (2001) *The Women's Suffrage Movement: a Reference Guide 1866-1928*. England: Routledge.

Edlin-White, R. (2017) *Helen Kirkpatrick Watts 1881-1972, Nottingham Suffragette*. Nottingham: Smallprint

Edlin-White, R. (2007) *Spinster of No Occupation? Mary Ellen Shaw: 1859-1926*. Nottingham: Smallprint.

Hammond C. I. (2012) *Architects, Angels, Activists and the City of Bath*. England: Ashgate Press.

Hawksley, L. (2013) *March, Women, March*. Andre Deutsch.

Holton, S. S. 'National Union of Women's Suffrage Societies (act 1896-1918)', *Oxford Dictionary of National Biography*. England: Oxford University Press, England. Accessed 5/4/2015.

Holton, S. S. 'Women's Social and Political Union (act.1903-1914)', *Oxford Dictionary of National Biography*. England: Oxford University Press. Accessed 5/4/2015

Hunt C. (2014) *The National Federation of Women Workers 1906-1921*. Available as an e-book

Liddington, J. (2006) *Rebel Girls: their fight for the vote*. London: Virago

Liddington, J. (2014) *Vanishing for the Vote: suffrage, citizenship and the battle for the census*. England: Manchester University Press.

Meynell, Dame A. (1988) *Public Servant, Private Woman*. London: Gollancz

Meynell, Dame A. (1998) *What Grandmother Said: The Life of Alice Dowson 1844-1927* based on her diaries. Cambridge: Colt

1911 Census (2015) 'Why can't I find my ancestor?' [online] Available at http://www.1911census.co.uk/Content/default.aspx?r=24

Wyncoll P. (1985) *The Nottingham Labour Movement 1880-1939*. London: Lawrence and Wishart Ltd.

Further Reading

Adams, J. (2014) *Women and the Vote, a World History*. England: Oxford University Press.

Herbert M. (2012) *Up Then Brave Women: Manchester's Radical Women 1819-1918*. England: North West Labour History Society.

Pugh M. (2008) *The Pankhursts: The History of One Radical Family*. London: Vintage Press.

Pugh M. (2000) *The March of the Women: A Revisionist Analysis of the Campaign for Women's Suffrage 1866-1914*. England: Oxford University Press.

Tickner, L. (1989) *The Spectacle of Women: Imagery of the Suffrage Campaign 1907-14*. London: Chatto & Windus.

Index

Acland, F D, Liberal MP, 38, 39
Actresses Franchise League, 62
Ainsworth, Laura, 23
Albert Hall, Nottm, 23, 26, 38
Anderson, Elizabeth Garrett, 29
Armstrong, Rev Richard, 9, 18
Artists' Suffrage League, 61
Ashton, Margaret, 22
Asquith, Herbert, Liberal MP, 17, 23, 26, 30, 35, 36, 48, 58
Babbington Colliery fire, 49, 50
Baines, Mrs, 23
Baker, Annie – see Lees
Banners, 46
Barrett, Rachel, 15, 22, 75
Barringer, Louisa Maria, 41, 74
Basford Board of Guardians, 64
Beaver, Miss I, 45
Becker, Lydia, 10
Biggs, Caroline, 10
Black, Clementina, 41
'Black Friday', 30, 67
Blandy, Mrs W H, 42, 74
Blathwayte family, 71
Britannia Boat House, burning of, 40
British Women's Temperance Soc, 9, 64
Brook, Mrs, 11
Brownsword, Anderson, 8, 57
Brownsword, Jeanie, 57
Brownsword, Helena – see Dowson
Bulcote barn fire, 49, 50
Bulwell, 37, 47, 49
Burgis, Catherine Mary 'May', 14, 34, 36, 53-54, 68, 74
Burgis, Miss E, 62
Butler, Mrs, 11
Calvert's Café, Long Row, 29
Canterbury, Archbishop of, 47
Carey, Henrietta, 7, 67
Carpenter, Edward, 22, 58
Casey, Eileen, 50, 51
'Cat and Mouse Act', 38, 39, 47
Census Boycott 1911, 31ff, 36, 53, 61, 63, 67, 70

Chartism, 5
Chesterfield, 45
Chomely, Mr, MLWS, 46
Church League for Women's Suffrage (CLWS) Nottm, 18, 28, 29, 67
Churchill, Winston, 22, 23, 70
Circus St Hall – see East Circus St. Hall
Clarendon School for Girls, 53
Clarion Club, 14
Cobbe, Frances Power, 9
Common Cause, The, NUWSS paper, 45
Co-operative Hall, Nottm, 10
Corn Exchange, Nottm, 40
Cotton, Henry, Liberal MP, 28
Cowen, Ann *nee* Guilford, 8, 19, 11,
Cowen, Mr E S, 11
Craigen, Jessie, 10
Crocker, Ellen, 'Nellie', 22, 23, 24, 30, 34, 35, 36, 37, 44, 75
Crook, Miss, 28
Cropper, Mr H S, 11
Davidson, Emily Wilding, 61
Dax, Alice Mary *nee* Mills, 55-56
Dax, Henry Richard, 55
Despard, Charlotte, 18
D'Hersant, Mrs, 11
Dickens, Mary Angela, 23
Direct Action in Nottm, 35ff, 48-50
Downing, Helena, 10
Dowson, Alice, 8, 10, 12, 19, 23, 30, 31, 35, 52, 57, 74
Dowson, Benjamin, 57
Dowson, Helena 'Nellie', 8, 9, 12, 20, 22, 24, 25, 28, 31, 42, 43, 46, 50, 57-59, 64, 74
Dowson, Hilda, 28, 31, 57, 74
Dowson, Lina, 57
Dowson, Maud, 19, 22, 23, 28, 31, 57-59, 74
Dowson, William Enfield, 57, 58
Drummond, Flora, 21
Eagle House, Batheaston, 71
East Circus St. Hall, 17, 19, 39, 69

E. Midland Federation of NUWSS, 29, 31, 43, 45, 46; Fete 1912, 66, 67
E. Nottm Women's Liberal Assn, 59
Eastwood, 55, 56
Eastern Counties Federations NUWSS, 45
Fabian Society, 20
Fairfield, Dr Letitia, 28
Family Care, 66
Fawcett, Millicent Garrett, 7, 12, 15, 23, 24, 25, 29, 41, 45, 51
Female Cigar Workers Union, 25
Female Lace Workers' Society, 25
Finningley, 60
Forest Recreation Ground, 19, 20
Friends of Women's Suffrage, 36
'From Prison to Citizenship' 1910, 28
Garrett, Agnes, 9
General Elections 1910, 26ff, 51, 58
Gilbert, Ann Taylor, 6
Gillick, Kate Eleanor, 34
Girls' Evening Home Movement, 66
Goodcliffe, Mrs, 74
Gosling, Mrs, 25
Graham, Mary Henrietta, 63
Grantham, 46
Greenhall, Miss, 34, 74
Greig, Teresa Billington, 18
Guild of Helpers, 68
Guilford, Hannah, 8, 11, 74
Harberton, Lady Florence, 11
Hallett, Lilias Ashworth, 9
Hall, Elsie, 30, 74
Hamilton, Cicely, 62
Handford, Mrs, 42
Harley, Katherine, 45
Hawkins, Alice, 21, 23
Hickling, Lillian Maud, 30, 74
Hill, Mrs F E *nee* Mayer, 75
Hilton, Enid *nee* Hopkin, 55-56
Hind, Mr & Mrs Jesse, 11
Hinscliffe, Rev Claude, 28, 29
Hinscliffe, Gertrude, 29
Holmes, Marion, *nee* Milner, 44
Hopkin, William & Sallie, 55, 56
Hoskyns Bishop Edwyn, 42
Hoskyns, Mrs Mary, 42, 74
How-Martin, Edith, 32

Howey, Elsie, 60-61, 71, 75
Howey, Gertrude *nee* Oldfield, 60-61
Howey, Mary, 60-61, 71, 75
Hucknall, 43, 64
Hucknall Labour Party, 4
Hucknall NUWSS, 43
Hucknall Women's Adult School, 43, 65
Hutchinson, Sarah, 34, 75
Hyde Park, 45, 46
Ilkeston, 36
Independent Labour Party, Nottm, 14
Joan of Arc, 60, 61
Justices of the Peace (JPs), women as, 8, 41, 59
Keevil, Gladice, 15, 21, 22
Kenney, Annie, 39, 47, 55
Kenney, Nell, 21
Lace Finishers Branch, 25
Lamb, Aeta, 17
Lancashire & Cheshire Textile & Other Workers Representation Committee, 13
Lawrence D H, 55, 56
League of the Church Militant – see CLWS, 29
League of Nations Union, 65
Lees, Edith Annie, 36, 62-63, 75
Lees, John Martin, 62-63
Leicester Gaol, 70
Leicester WSPU, 23, 70
Leif-Jones, L S, Liberal MP, 38
Lloyd George, David, 26, 48, 51
Lloyd Thomas, Rev J M, 18
London National Society for Women's Suffrage, Nottm, 9
Long Bennington, 46
Long Eaton, 39
Lucas, Margaret Bright, 9
Lytton, Lady Constance, 29
Macarthur, Mary, 25, 26
Mallett, Mrs C, 41
Manhood Suffrage Bill, 36
Manners, Emily, 8, 41, 45, 46, 74
Manning School for Girls, 54
Mansfield, 37, 41, 45, 56
Mansfield Junior Suffrage Society, 42
Mansfield NUWSS, 42, 46
Mansfield Women's Liberal Assn, 41

Mansfield Women's Suffrage Society, 41ff
Markham, A B, Liberal MP, 41
Markham, Mrs, 41
Marsh, Charlotte, 23, 37, 75
Martel, Nellie Alma, 21
Massey, Simon, 67
Mayer, Julie, 75
McKee, Rev Robert, 43
McLaren, Priscilla Bright, 9
Mechanics Institute, Nottm, 16, 23, 28, 58, 69
Mee, Annie Ellen, *nee* Baker, 62
Mee, Charles Joseph, 62
Men's League for Women's Suffrage (MLWS), 18, 19
Merrick, Joseph William, 64
Merrick, Sarah Barker, 43, 64-65, 74
Meynell, Dame Alex, 52
Mollison, Kathleen, 37
Morley, Arnold, MP, 10
Morley Club, Nottm, 10
Morley's Café, Wheeler Gate, 22, 24, 67, 70
Morrison, James, Unionist MP, 26
Moss, William, Labour Councillor, 64
Movement for the Ordination of Women (MOW), 29
Municipal Distress Committee, 42
National Council of Women, 63, 67
National Federation of Women Workers (NFWW), 25, 37
National Society for Women's Suffrage, 9, 10, 40
National Union of Practical Suffragists, 12
National Union of Railwaymen, 40
National Union of Women Workers, 7, 9, 66
National Union of Women's Suffrage Societies (NUWSS), 12, 30, 33, 36, 45, 58
National Women's Liberal Federation, 12
Neal, Mary Clara Sophia, 8
Nesbitt, Mrs, 44
Newark, 40, 45
Nottingham Boat Club, 39
Nottm Council, Resolution in Favour of Women's Suffrage, 1911, 62

Nottingham Efficiency Club, 63
Nottingham Female Hosiery Workers Union, 25
Nottingham Female Political Union, 5
Nottingham Labour Church, 8
Nottingham Ladies Society for the Relief of Negro Slaves, 6
Nottingham Liberal Union, 59
Nottingham NUWSS, 18, 19, 22, 23, 26, 28, 30, 39, 46
Nottingham School Board, 8
Nottingham Town & County Social Guild 1875, 7
Nottingham Trades Union Council, 14, 37
Nottingham Women's Suffrage Society, 11, 12, 13, 57
Nottingham WSPU, 14, 16, 17, 19, 21, 22, 23, 28, 35, 36, 47, 53, 67, 69
Onslow, Lady Madeline, 45
Oswald, Elsa, 28, 75
'Pageant of Great Women', 62
Pankhurst, Adela, 13, 28
Pankhurst, Christabel, 13, 14, 15, 16, 17, 18, 19, 20, 21, 51, 57, 67, 69
Pankhurst, Mrs Emmeline, 13, 14, 18, 19, 21, 22, 29, 36, 40, 51, 61, 71
Pankhurst, Sylvia, 13, 36, 47
'Peoples' Budget' 1910, 26
Penlow, Miss, 42
Peters, Miss, 26, 37
Pethick, Dorothy, 14, 28, 36, 75
Pethick Lawrence, Emmeline, 14, 16, 21, 36, 60
Pethick Lawrence, Frederick, 36
Pleasley & Pleasley Hill, 45
Pleasley Colliery Band, 45
Plumed Serpent, The, 56
Poor Law Amendment Act 1834, 5
Poor Law Guardians, women as, 8, 41, 57, 64, 66
Prisoners (Temporary Discharge for Ill Health) Act 1913 – see Cat and Mouse
Radcliffe, Mary Ann (1746-1818), 6
Rathbone, Eleanor, 22, 58
Rawson, Mary, 22, 70, 75
Redmond, John, IPP, 26
Representation of the People Act 1918, 52

Retford, 44
Retford WSPU, 44
Ridding, Bishop George, 7, 65-66
Ridding, Lady Laura *nee* Palmer, 7, 65-66
Roberts, Gladys, 35, 44, 75
Roberts, Ursula, 29
Roll of Honour of Suffragette Prisoners 1905-1914, 63; Nottingham Roll, 74-75
Rothera, Charles L, 19, 47, 67
Samuels, Mrs, 11
Saint Mary's Church, Bulwell, 47
Saint Mary's Church Nottm. 47
Sandford, Mrs, 7
Scratcherd, Alice Cliff, 10
Shaw, Leonora, 14, 34, 74
Shearer, Mrs, 11
Smith, Miss A, 11
Smith, Dudley Stewart, Liberal MP, 28
Smith Norma, 43, 46
Smith, Valentia, 42, 43, 74
Snowden, Ethel *nee* Annakin, 28
'Socialist', 43
Sons and Lovers, 56
Southwell, 42, 45, 65
Southwell NUWSS, 42
Stanger, Henry, Liberal MP, 19
Stansbury, Mrs, 19, 46
Sterling, Frances, 28
Shops, NUWSS & WSPU, Nottm, 15, 22, 39, 58; Hucknall, 43, 64; Retford, 44
'Suffrage Sunday', 20
Suffragette Fellowship, 71, 73
'Suffragettes', origin of name, 15
'Suffragettes' Wood', 71
Sunter, Elizabeth, 9, 11
Taylor, Helen, 10
Taylor, Jane, 6
Teschemacher, Mrs, 11
Thorpe, Mary, 75
'Uncle Tom', 44
'United Procession of Women' 1907, 15
United Religious League 1913 – see CLWS, 29
University College, Nottm, 15, 16
Victoria Hall, Nottm, 22
Violent protest by Nottm WSPU, 35-40
Votes for Women newspaper, 13, 20, 21

Wainwright, Ethel, 74
Wallis, Mrs, 74
Wallis, George Harry, FSA, 67
Wallis, Katherine Watson *nee* Carey, 67
Wallis, Muriel, 30, 34, 67-68, 75
Watts, Rev Alan Hunter, 18, 22, 69-71
Watts, Alice Margaret, 34, 70, 74
Watts, Ethelinda 'Ethel' Bertha, 69, 71, 74
Watts, Ethelinda Woodrow *nee* Cassels, 69, 70
Watts, Helen Kirkpatrick, 22-24, 34, 36, 69-71, 75
Watts, Nevile Hunter, 69
West Midlands Federation of NUWSS, 31
Wilton, Miss, 74
Windley, Mr J W, 11
Women's Co-operative Guild, 36, 42
'Women's Coronation Procession', 35, 58
Women's Defence Relief Corps, 51
Women's Franchise (Conciliation Bill) 1910, 28, 30, 32, 35, 58
Women's Freedom League, 18, 32, 33
Women's Industrial Council, 41
Women's Liberal Federation, 12, 15, 26
Women's Social & Political Union (WSPU), 13, 18, 30, 32, 33 – see also Nottingham WSPU
Women's Suffrage Pilgrimage 1913, 42, 43, 45-47, 59
Women's Tax Resistance League (WTRL), 32
Women's Temperance Society - see also British Women's Temperance Soc, 9
Women's Total Abstinence Union, 41
World War 1, 42, 51-52
Wright, Louisa, 11, 41, 45, 74
Young, Esther, 25, 37
Yates, Thomas Lamartine, 63
Young Women's Christian Assn (YWCA), 66, 68
Yoxall, Sir James, Liberal MP, 23, 26, 38
Yoxall, Lady, 46
Zimmern, Alice Louisa Theodora, 72
Zimmern, family, 72

81

Acknowledgments

With thanks to all of you who have contributed to this project, especially to Margaret Rizk, who shared her own extensive research with us; to Susan Taylor, who shared information about her grandmother, Edith Annie Lees, and allowed us reproduce material from her scrapbook; to Elizabeth Crawford for permission to use the image on the front cover; and to Jill Liddington and Cynthia Imogen Hammond for their interest and encouragement.

We are especially grateful to the Watts family who lent us Helen Watts' suffrage scrapbook which enabled us to add further information to this edition of *No Surrender!* and continue to encourage us in our research.

As always, we wish to acknowledge the invaluable help of Nottinghamshire Archives and the Nottingham Local History Library, Angel Row.

Image from *Punch*, 1917

Helen Kirkpatrick Watts

Nottingham Suffragette

1881-1972

An illustrated 20-page pamphlet dedicated to Helen Kirkpatrick Watts.

Published by *Smallprint*. ISBN: 978-1-900074-30-8 £2.00.
Available at nottinghambooks.co.uk or contact ro@edlin-white.net